Cambridge Elements

Elements in Applied Linguistics
edited by
Li Wei
University College London
Zhu Hua
University College London

DISCOURSE, MATERIALITY, AND AGENCY WITHIN EVERYDAY SOCIAL INTERACTIONS

Dariush Izadi
Western Sydney University

Shaftesbury Road, Cambridge CB2 8EA, United Kingdom

One Liberty Plaza, 20th Floor, New York, NY 10006, USA

477 Williamstown Road, Port Melbourne, VIC 3207, Australia

314–321, 3rd Floor, Plot 3, Splendor Forum, Jasola District Centre,
New Delhi – 110025, India

103 Penang Road, #05–06/07, Visioncrest Commercial, Singapore 238467

Cambridge University Press is part of Cambridge University Press & Assessment,
a department of the University of Cambridge.

We share the University's mission to contribute to society through the pursuit of
education, learning and research at the highest international levels of excellence.

www.cambridge.org
Information on this title: www.cambridge.org/9781009675376

DOI: 10.1017/9781009675390

© Dariush Izadi 2025

This publication is in copyright. Subject to statutory exception and to the provisions
of relevant collective licensing agreements, no reproduction of any part may take
place without the written permission of Cambridge University Press & Assessment.

When citing this work, please include a reference to the DOI 10.1017/9781009675390

First published 2025

A catalogue record for this publication is available from the British Library

ISBN 978-1-009-67537-6 Hardback
ISBN 978-1-009-67536-9 Paperback
ISSN 2633-5069 (online)
ISSN 2633-5050 (print)

Cambridge University Press & Assessment has no responsibility for the persistence
or accuracy of URLs for external or third-party internet websites referred to in
this publication and does not guarantee that any content on such websites is, or
will remain, accurate or appropriate.

For EU product safety concerns, contact us at Calle de José Abascal, 56, 1°, 28003
Madrid, Spain, or email eugpsr@cambridge.org

Discourse, Materiality, and Agency within Everyday Social Interactions

Elements in Applied Linguistics

DOI: 10.1017/9781009675390
First published online: November 2025

Dariush Izadi
Western Sydney University
Author for correspondence: Dariush Izadi, D.Izadi@westernsydney.edu.au

Abstract: This Element investigates the interplay between language, discourse, and materiality by focusing on everyday social practices within corner shops and markets in Sydney, Australia. Drawing on linguistic ethnography and data from interactions involving objects, talk, and people, it explores how discourse and materiality are co-constituted. Employing theoretical perspectives from actor-network theory and the concept of mediational means/tools, the study reconceptualizes the role of non-human entities in meaning-making processes. It demonstrates that objects actively participate in shaping cultural practices and social dynamics, offering new insights that broaden applied linguistics' engagement with materiality. By treating objects as agents in discourse, this Element highlights the entanglement of language, agency, and the material world. It foregrounds the dynamic relationships between humans and non-humans in everyday communicative practices, bringing to the fore the significance of material conditions in the production of meaning and interaction.

Keywords: mediational tools, material culture, actant, agency, language and materiality

© Dariush Izadi 2025

ISBNs: 9781009675376 (HB), 9781009675369 (PB), 9781009675390 (OC)
ISSNs: 2633-5069 (online), 2633-5050 (print)

Contents

1 Introduction   1

2 Methodology and Analytical Tools   19

3 Objects as Mediators in the Semiotic Landscape   23

4 Material Objects and Institutional Agency in Practice   27

5 Entangling Discourse, Materiality, and Identity in Diasporic Service Encounters   44

6 Conclusion   65

   References   69

1 Introduction

During a visit to a Persian shop in Sydney, I observed a conversation that illustrated the role of everyday objects in shaping social interactions. A regular customer, a general practitioner (GP), was discussing the health benefits of fresh vegetables, comparing his experiences in Iran with those in Australia. He explained how, in Iran, families often pick fresh vegetables from their gardens, emphasising their nutritional value, their richness in fibre, and their role in preventing chronic diseases such as heart disease. He highlighted the challenges of accessing such fresh produce and suggested shops like this Persian one play a crucial role in providing quality vegetables. While this might initially seem like a simple exchange about food, it reflects broader concerns. Everyday objects such as vegetables serve more than merely functional purposes; they mediate interpersonal relations and participate in broader discourses, including those surrounding health, cultural identity, and migration. This moment raises important questions: how do everyday objects mediate social relations? What role do they play in identity constructions and cultural practices? Can seemingly mundane everyday objects such as vegetables act as agents (also known as actants, see further) within networks of discourse, shaping and reflecting social dynamics?

To begin unpacking these questions, I turn to a site that is both analytically rich and personally meaningful. This Persian shop is not just a field site, but a space that resonates with my own personal and cultural identity. As someone of Persian background, I have long been familiar with this shop and its community. It serves not only as a place of commerce, but as a cultural and social hub where language, food, and identity converge in meaningful ways (Izadi, 2017, 2020, 2023; Lou, 2017). Many of my participants expressed that the shop reminded them of 'home', evoking sensory and emotional ties to their lives in Iran. This aligns with Zhu Hua, Li Wei, and Lyons' (2017) concept of the 'node', that is, a physical or symbolic space where translocal and translingual practices gather and are reconfigured. In this sense, the shop becomes a node of cultural continuity and identity negotiation for diasporic individuals navigating multiple socio-cultural worlds.

My connection to this site is shaped by a dual positionality: I draw on both an insider's cultural familiarity (emic) and a reflexive, analytical stance as a researcher. While I maintain a critical distance in my analysis, this familiarity allows me to notice subtle cues, codes, and cultural references that might otherwise go unnoticed. Ethnographers have long emphasised the importance of engagement with research sites in order to understand what matters to community members (Hammersley & Atkinson, 2019). Building on this,

Sarangi (2007) introduces the notion of 'thick participation', following Geertz's (1973) 'thick description', highlighting how immersion can help identify socially and culturally meaningful practices. This study is grounded in that methodological ethos, drawing on a social semiotic perspective and analytical tools from Mediated Discourse Analysis (MDA) (Norris & Jones, 2005; Scollon, 2001), to trace how everyday objects function in socially mediated activity.

Building on these methodological and conceptual foundations, I return to the broader questions raised earlier: objects are not merely passive elements in our surroundings; rather, they are active participants in meaning-making and social relations. Objects, from everyday items to culturally symbolic artefacts to even abstract thoughts and concepts (Norris, 2004), play a crucial, yet often overlooked, role in mediating social practices, cultural meanings, and identity through their semiotic and material agency (Appadurai, 2015; Latour, 1996a, 1996b, 2005; Sayes, 2014). Drawing from Actor-Network Theory (ANT, see further), objects are conceptualised not as inert tools, but as actants, that is, entities that can initiate or modify action within networks of relations (Latour, 2005). As Scollon (2001) explains, they act as mediational means/tools that facilitate and shape how people engage with and interpret their cultural environments. For instance, an open box of fruit dates in a Persian shop may symbolise a religious ritual for a Persian-speaking customer, while serving as a sensory evaluation for an Anglo-Australian (Izadi, 2020). Despite their frequent invisibility in daily life, objects profoundly embody and influence societal structures, power dynamics, and identity formations through their culturally specific uses (Kopytoff, 1986; Miller, 2005). Recognising the agency of objects is key to understanding their central role in constructing everyday social and cultural experiences, a role that is often overlooked.

To explore these questions further, this Element draws on frameworks such as ANT, MDA, material culture studies, and posthumanist applied linguistics to examine how objects, such as the vegetables in the Persian shop, function as active agents in shaping social identity, cultural practices, and transnational connections. These theoretical approaches highlight the complex interplay between materiality and discourse, showing how objects mediate social interactions and contribute to the construction of cultural norms and social relationships. In doing so, they challenge traditional distinctions between language and materiality, subject and object, and instead foreground the relational and distributed nature of agency. In the following sections, I first ground this discussion by elaborating on the concept of 'nonhuman' actants within ANT, which provides a critical framework for understanding how objects operate as active participants in social networks. I will then explore the entanglements of materiality and language, drawing on insights from MDA and material culture studies, followed by an analysis of Deleuze and Guattari's (1987) concept of assemblages, to better understand how materiality and agency function within dynamic social and cultural contexts.

1.1 Nonhuman Mediation and Cultural Identity

This section explores how nonhuman entities such as shop objects, commodities, and infrastructures act as mediators of cultural identity and belonging in diasporic spaces. Drawing on ANT and complementary frameworks such as MDA and material culture studies, I argue that objects are not passive carriers of meaning but active participants in shaping diasporic social life. ANT advances this perspective through the concept of the 'nonhuman', entities such as tools (Latour & Woolgar, 1986), texts (Callon, 1984), animals (Cornips, 2024; Cornips & van Koppen, 2024; Latour, 1993), infrastructure, and commodities (Callon, 1999), that exert influence within social networks. These elements, once considered inert, are redefined as mediators of meaning and practice. ANT thus unsettles anthropocentric understandings of agency while still maintaining a distinction between subjects and objects (Sayes, 2012, 2014). The 'nonhuman' fits within a broader ANT vocabulary, alongside notions such as 'quasi-object' and 'hybrid' (Latour, 1993, p. 117), and emphasises the roles of those elements that actively shape social relations without being human. Latour's (1987, 1996a, 1996b, 2005) notion of the 'actant' extends this idea further, referring to any entity capable of generating effects, and shifting analytical attention from intention to material arrangements.

ANT (Latour, 1996a, 1996b, 2005) therefore offers a valuable framework for examining how both material and linguistic elements, as actants, shape the negotiation of belonging and identity in diasporic markets. By viewing agency as an emergent property of networks involving heterogeneous elements (Sayes, 2014), ANT repositions everyday objects as co-constructors of social life. For example, the vegetables displayed in Persian grocery shops are not merely commodities; they function as nonhuman actants that actively shape cultural identity and transnational connections. Their visibility, placement, and circulation participate in social interactions, helping to construct and sustain diasporic belonging. Within this network, such objects can act as what Alfred Gell (1998) calls social agents, that is, entities that mediate human relationships and cultural values, rather than merely reflecting them.

Extending this understanding, it becomes important to differentiate the distinct roles objects can play in shaping interaction. Some primarily operate as cultural symbols that surface in talk, for instance, particular ways of cooking rice, which may evoke nostalgic memories or regional affiliations. Others materially mediate interaction by shaping the physical and social environment: the layout of goods, the presence of culturally resonant decor, or the tactility of packaging can influence how people move, speak, and relate within the space. These forms of mediation enrich our understanding of objects as actants within assemblages, where human and nonhuman entities dynamically co-construct meaning and social practice (Pennycook, 2018a, 2018b). Rather than treating objects as isolated agents, this approach locates them within relational networks that intertwine talk, materiality, and affect. This perspective is supported by material culture studies (Miller, 2005) and complements MDA (Norris & Jones, 2005; Scollon, 2001), which highlights how discourse is one of many mediational means (Norris, 2004; Norris & Jones, 2005; Scollon, 2001; Wertsch, 1998) through which people engage with the material world. In this view, practices like rice preparation (Izadi, 2017) or display are not just culinary routines but semiotic and social mediators embedded in broader networks of cultural reproduction and meaning-making. Tracing how such nonhuman elements participate in discourse and everyday practices enables a richer understanding of the entanglement of materiality, agency, and identity.

For Latour (1996a, 1996b), this shift from physical separation to relational connections challenges the 'tyranny of distance', arguing that geographical boundaries matter less than the relationships formed between entities. This understanding of 'connection' highlights the importance of relational interactions across scales, whether global or local, in shaping meanings and practices within networks. This rethinking of agency also requires us to reconceive spatiality not as distance to be overcome, but as a web of relations continually reassembled through actants. A key process within ANT, translation (Latour, 1996a), facilitates the reconfiguration of relationships between actants, enabling the extension and transformation of networks. In diasporic shops, for instance, the act of purchasing an imported herb is not just a local exchange but a reactivation of global relationalities through the process of translation. Translation allows us to understand how diasporic customer practices instantiate distant connections and render abstract networks tangible. Objects like product packaging or pricing labels are not neutral; they mediate diasporic identities and activate transnational cultural imaginaries. Thus, in diasporic markets, translation helps us understand how customer behaviours, product designs, and cultural norms interact and evolve, reshaping both local and global consumption networks.

Sayes (2014) critically explores what it means to attribute agency to nonhumans. To better understand how such relational connections unfold in practice, especially in spaces like diasporic markets, I turn to Sayes' (2014) articulation of nonhuman agency within ANT. His approach allows us to more precisely articulate how objects not only enable connection, but also anchor, mediate, moralise, and temporally reconfigure social life. Building on his framework, I take 'nonhumans' not simply as material things or background conditions but as dynamic participants in social processes whose presence and capacities shape collective life. I understand nonhuman contributions in four interrelated ways, drawn from ANT and its key thinkers, following Sayes (2014, pp. 137–141): (1) as conditions of sociality, (2) as mediators of meaning and action, (3) as participants in moral-political assemblages, and (4) as carriers of temporality and memory.

First, nonhumans are a condition for the very possibility of human society. Drawing on Callon and Latour's (Callon & Latour, 1981) notion of the 'Monkey-Leviathan', ANT contrasts human society with primate groups such as baboons to argue that human macro-social orders depend not just on symbolic exchange, but on the involvement of durable material elements. Machines, documents, infrastructures, and other artefacts stabilise social relations by outlasting the ephemeral interactions that created them (Callon & Latour, 1981, pp. 283–284; Latour, 1993). ANT thus shifts emphasis from intersubjectivity to inter-objectivity, highlighting how durable nonhuman elements stabilise the ephemeral nature of social interaction. In the Persian shop I observed in Sydney, nonhumans like the arrangement of herbs, bulk sacks of rice, or the scent of barberries and dried limes similarly endure, creating a spatial memory that anchors interactions and stabilises a sense of continuity. These elements outlast conversations and transactions, embedding a sense of cultural familiarity.

Second, nonhumans do not merely transmit human intentions; they mediate and transform them. While early ANT sometimes treated objects as intermediaries – entities that simply convey force without altering it, subsequent formulations emphasise their status as mediators (Callon, 1991; Latour, 1999; Latour & Venn, 2002). Mediators reconfigure the relations they traverse, producing effects that exceed intentional design. From scallops (Callon, 1984) to ocean currents (Law, 1987), ANT studies show that nonhumans act not as neutral tools, but as transformative agents embedded in and shaping social networks. As Latour puts it, 'objects are not means, but rather mediators, just as other actors are' (Latour, 1996c, p. 240).Their agency is contingent, emergent, and relational. For example, in the Persian store, the presence of an imported soft drink refrigerator decorated with the pre-revolutionary Iranian flag (from the Pahlavi era) subtly transforms the shop space into a politically and emotionally layered site. Such mediations are often unnoticed yet potent, embedding political affects and nostalgic imaginaries into mundane consumer encounters. The flag, which may go unnoticed by some, mediates a nostalgic connection to a particular version of Iranian identity that precedes the 1979 revolution and in turn reshapes the experience of the shop as more than just a commercial site. It becomes a carrier of memory, loss, and alternative national imaginaries.

Importantly, ANT disentangles intentionality from agentive potential, emphasising the effects that actants have within a network. This shift moves the focus from human-centred notions of agency to a more distributed understanding, where material objects are recognised as actants that mediate social practices, identity formation, and consumer behaviour. Scollon's (Scollon, 2013, pp. 185, emphasis in original) notion of 'ACTION THROUGH THE USE OF OBJECTS' emphasises how meaning is produced through the interplay of human and non-human actants (see also Jocuns & Groot, 2025). In the context of diasporic markets, this dynamic is particularly evident in how products, advertising, shop layouts, and broader cultural trends influence consumer choices and behaviours, demonstrating how material objects and language interact to shape social relations and cultural values. These ANT-informed insights reveal how consumer behaviour is co-constituted by linguistic and material actants, offering a textured understanding of diasporic cultural life.

Third, nonhumans are enrolled in moral and political associations. Technologies such as seatbelts or warning buzzers materialise norms and ethical expectations. By limiting choices or shaping normative expectations, nonhumans operate as components of ethical and political life (Callon, 1991, p. 157). Rather than anthropomorphising objects, ANT challenges the idea that morality or politics are exclusively human domains, instead arguing that agency is distributed across assemblages of human and nonhuman actants (Latour, 1987, 1999, pp. 192–193). The prominent placement of goods like saffron, rosewater, or prayer rugs similarly materialises ethical and religious orientations, transforming shelf space into moral and affective terrain. These items carry implicit messages about taste, piety, respectability, or nostalgia, embedding moral dispositions within everyday acts of consumption.

Finally, nonhumans act as condensations of multiple temporalities and distributed relations. Responding to critiques that attributing agency to objects flattens human distinctiveness, ANT reframes action as emergent from relational networks that span people, times, and places (Callon, 1991; Latour, 1992; Latour & Venn, 2002). A single artefact, say, a branded bag of herbs, can condense distant agricultural practices, migratory memories, regulatory infrastructures, and intimate forms of care. These objects gather and transport heterogeneous temporalities: the time of harvesting, the time of exile, the time of cooking, and the time of remembrance. Latour and Venn (2002) describe such entities not as inert residues of the past, but as durable nodes through which social time is assembled and felt. In the diasporic market, they weave a chronotope (Karimzad & Catedral, 2021) by bringing together harvest time, diasporic rhythms, and the everyday temporality of domestic use.

Taken together, these four dimensions of nonhuman agency reconceptualise the shop not merely as a commercial or cultural site but as a complex mediational field where talk, identity, memory, and materiality are co-assembled. By attending to everyday objects, fridges, packaging, and scents, we uncover how diasporic lives are lived through the active participation of nonhuman actants, enacting identity not only through discourse or representation but through material entanglements that exceed the human. Sayes' fourfold model serves as a heuristic entry point, but must be situated within the affective, contradictory, and contested realities of everyday practice. In this Element, I therefore deploy Sayes' (2014) categories as a generative entry point, re-embedded in the lived textures of diasporic practice, where memory, political longing, and identity are materially enacted, contested, and reconfigured. This critical extension foregrounds the emergent and sometimes unstable nature of nonhuman agency, and it points toward a broader understanding in which language, like objects, functions as an agent in negotiating cultural belonging. Ultimately, unpacking these material-semiotic entanglements is essential to grasping how diasporic identities are constructed and lived through both objects and linguistic practices.

1.2 Material-Semiotic Practices and the Affective Life of Diaspora

Following from this material-semiotic perspective, Sara Ahmed's (2014) concept of 'sticky objects' provides a useful lens for understanding how certain material entities in diasporic spaces such as packaging or shop interiors become saturated with emotional and affective attachments. These objects, Ahmed (2014) argues, do not merely signify belonging; they enact belonging through their capacity to accumulate and circulate affect, often tied to shared histories and embodied memories. In diasporic markets, such 'stickiness' is not incidental but constitutive of how social attachments are maintained and identities are co-constructed. These shifting relations between people, objects, signs, and environments reflect the actor-network approach, where agency emerges from assemblages rather than individual agents, reinforcing Latour's (2005) notion that agency is always a property of an association.

This affective-material dynamic is further illuminated by empirical research. Dovchin's (2021) study on Mongolian-background ESL women in Australia illustrates how translanguaging beyond the classroom creates emotionally and linguistically safe spaces that help manage psychological distress. These affective practices unfold in socially and materially mediated environments – homes, community hubs, and other informal diasporic settings – that closely mirror the sensory and emotive atmospheres of diasporic shops. Crucially, Dovchin's findings resonate with Ahmed's (2014) notion of 'sticky objects', demonstrating how such spaces and artefacts become emotionally charged and function as stabilisers of identity and well-being. This kind of empirical insight reinforces the need to examine how material-semiotic practices contribute not only to identity formation but also to the emotional and embodied lives of diasporic subjects.

Extending this idea, recent posthumanist work in applied linguistics (Auger & Dervin, 2021; Badwan & Hall, 2020; Hopkyns, 2025; Kebabi, 2024; Pennycook, 2018a) emphasises how the entanglement of affect, space, and materiality disrupts human-centric models of identity formation. Hopkyns' (2025) notion of 'material-discursive practices' in English Medium Instruction contexts, and Badwan and Hall's walk-along methodology, highlight how emotional resonance with spaces and objects, that is, what they term 'sticky places', can foster intersubjective meaning-making and intercultural understanding. Kebabi (2024) similarly foregrounds non-human actors (naming practices, food, death) in shaping 'identity', using posthumanist theory to argue for an expanded ontology of the self that includes affective and symbolic relations with material artefacts. These insights support a broader rethinking of agency – one that treats objects not merely as containers of meaning but as affective and semiotic agents participating in the ongoing negotiation of cultural belonging. The 'stickiness' of objects, then, is not a metaphorical flourish but a critical analytic, helping us grasp how diasporic identities are lived, felt, and mediated through the textures of everyday life.

In diasporic markets, the materiality of language through labels, packaging, shop signs, and spoken interactions (Barnes, 2017) operates in tandem with physical objects such as traditional spices, textiles, or cookware to construct and negotiate belonging. As theorised in geolinguistics and studies of spatial repertoires (Aronin & Ó Laoire, 2013; Blackledge & Creese, 2017; Canagarajah, 2018; Pennycook & Otsuji, 2015; Ros i Solé, 2025; Scollon & Scollon, 2003), these communicative practices are shaped by spatially distributed material resources. While earlier we focused on the active role of objects, we now turn to how language, too, is embedded within political-economic structures that shape cultural identity (Shankar & Cavanaugh, 2017). By foregrounding the material dimensions of both objects and discourse, we move beyond viewing language as an abstract system. Instead, we recognise language as a practical material activity (Williams, 1977 in Shankar & Cavanaugh, 2017), deeply entwined with its conditions of production and exchange.

Just as the linguistic and material elements of diasporic markets shape identity and belonging, Thurlow's (2016) critical discourse analysis of elite airplane travel demonstrates how material objects, such as luxury amenities, and embodied practices jointly construct social distinction. This intersection between language and materiality mediates access and social stratification across different contexts. Similarly, in the case of the Persian shop, purchasing traditional spices engages participants in multisensory ways, where language and materiality converge to mediate cultural identity and foster social connections (Izadi, 2017; Ros i Solé, 2025). These interactions are not merely transactional but deeply affective, grounding individuals in shared memories and cultural reference points. The act of buying spices thus becomes a site of relational meaning-making, where sensory cues, linguistic exchanges, and material artefacts work together to sustain a sense of diasporic belonging. The shop becomes a sensory-linguistic space, where every purchase is embedded within affective, social, and historical networks.

This convergence of materiality and discourse aligns with posthumanist approaches that shift attention away from human-centred understandings of language and agency. As Pennycook (2018b) notes, this aligns with the posthumanist question of 'how and why we have come to think about humans in particular ways, with particular boundaries between humans and other animals, humans and artefacts, humans and nature' (p. 445). These ideas echo the call for an embodied sociolinguistics, as proposed by Bucholtz and Hall (2016), which recognise 'the distribution of agency beyond language to include human bodies as well as nonhuman entities, such as animals, other living beings, material objects, and the physical world' (p. 184). Similarly, Mondada (2016) critiques the long-standing logocentric view of language, emphasising the need to integrate embodied and material dimensions into sociolinguistic enquiry. Taken together, these perspectives foreground a distributed view of agency, where language is not a privileged carrier of meaning but one modality among others within assemblages of communication. Posthumanist approaches (Auger & Dervin, 2021; Pennycook, 2018a) are particularly relevant here, as they offer a framework to challenge the human-centric view of agency, showing how nonhuman elements actively shape human practices and identity. These theoretical shifts necessitate rethinking fundamental concepts such as indexicality, discourse, and agency, as Bucholtz and Hall suggest (2016, p. 188). This reorientation invites us to read everyday diasporic interactions, whether through the scent of herbs or the feel of packaging, as constitutive moments of identity work that collapse the subject-object binary.

Building on this, we can more explicitly conceptualise these phenomena through terms such as 'thing-power' (Bennett, 2010) and 'semiotic assemblages'

(Pennycook, 2018a, 2018b), which illuminate the dynamic relationships between material objects, language, and social practices. Thing-power refers to the ability of objects to influence human actions and perceptions, not simply through symbolic representation but through their tangible, functional presence in social interactions (Ros i Solé, 2025). Semiotic assemblages (Pennycook, 2017), on the other hand, highlight how meaning emerges from the interaction of signs, bodies, and materials, creating a dynamic network where both human and nonhuman agents co-construct social realities. These ideas extend the concept of agency to encompass both the material and the semiotic, showing how objects are not just passive backdrops in human interactions but active participants in shaping identity, cultural belonging, and social practices (Lamb & Higgins, 2020). Posthumanist approaches extend these discussions by highlighting how human and nonhuman actors converge and conflict, dynamically reshaping cultural and material arrangements. Consumption in diasporic markets, then, emerges not merely as an economic activity but as an affective practice, wherein semiotic-material agents collaboratively shape social distinction, intimacy, and belonging. In this process, material aspects are not merely part of the conversation but actively shape and are shaped by these dialogues, influencing broader cultural and natural environments.

Turning from affective and semiotic assemblages to the biographical trajectories of objects, as objects accumulate meaning over time, they actively shape social dynamics and reinforce their role within broader affective and cultural networks. The biographical approach in material culture (Gosden & Marshall, 1999; Hoskins, 2006; Kopytoff, 1986) explains how objects gain significance through their historical trajectories, shaping both individual experiences and collective identities. This process fosters connections within communities, as material objects mediate cultural identity by linking individuals to traditional values and practices that might otherwise fade in diasporic contexts. In this sense, they not only embody cultural meaning but also function as tangible, dynamic agents that reinforce continuity in both individual and communal identity. For example, vegetables – seemingly mundane commodities – become crucial in diasporic identity work. Conversations about fresh produce enable individuals to articulate their heritage, reinforcing cultural identity in the face of displacement or change. These interactions reflect the concept of 'thing-power' (Bennett, 2010; Benso, 2000), demonstrating how material objects not only influence social dynamics but actively embody nonhuman agency in shaping human practices. In this context, 'thing-power' is not just about emotional resonance but also about the practical and functional role of objects in everyday life. They serve as anchors for cultural practices and social relations, reinforcing a sense of continuity. Through these interactions, material objects do more than mediate cultural practices; they also actively sustain social connections and ensure the transmission of cultural knowledge across generations and regions. Over time, this accumulation of meaning extends beyond cultural identity, opening up new ways to understand the role of objects in shaping health discourse. Through their layered biographies, even perishable goods like pistachios, nuts, and raisins become carriers of affect, heritage, and sensory memory, grounding diasporic subjects in both place and time.

Finally, transitioning from cultural belonging to embodied health practices, as these objects shape cultural identity, they also influence bodily practices and hexis (Bourdieu, 1977a) and perceptions of well-being, particularly in how diasporic communities negotiate health within new socio-economic environments. In this sense, material objects function as both cultural and bodily mediators (Latour, 2005), bridging identity and well-being in multicultural settings. This intersection provides a rich opportunity to explore how cultural identity is negotiated through everyday objects in multicultural settings (Cavanaugh, 2007; Izadi, 2015, 2019, 2020, 2023; Izadi & Luke, 2025). In contrast to earlier views where objects were seen as passive backdrops, material culture studies (Keane, 2001, 2003; Manning, 2017; Miller, 2005; Shankar, 2006) now recognise them as active agents that accumulate meaning over time. Through iterative engagement in daily routines, these objects come to structure perception, shape bodily habits (Ros i Solé, 2025), and regulate normative ideas of health. Through their continued interaction within cultural and social practices (Appadurai, 1986; Kopytoff, 1986) even humble vegetables become central to shaping dietary perceptions and promoting healthier lifestyles, particularly in contrast to the fast-paced Australian environment.

This shift highlights how material culture is not merely reflective of social life but constitutive of it. This interaction illustrates how 'things talk to us' (Daston, 2004) through their 'obdurate objecthood', referring to the idea that objects have a persistent presence that compels us to engage with them. In this way, things participate in the formation of human beings (Saurma-Jeltsch, 2010), shaping both our understanding of the world and our social relations. Thus, objects do not just carry meaning (see Section 1.1); they actively generate and sustain social connections. This perspective highlights the dialogic relationship between humans and objects and demonstrates how material entities are more than symbolic; they actively structure social practices and identity work (Hoskins, 2006). Pennycook's (2017) notion of 'semiotic assemblages' offers a complementary framework to this material-semiotic mediation, illustrating how bodies, materials, and signs interact within these assemblages to co-construct meaning and shape social relations. By weaving together materiality, semiotics, and social practice, we can better understand how everyday objects mediate interactions and reinforce cultural identity. Examining these processes reveals that everyday objects, through their material and semiotic agency, not only mediate social interactions but also structure lived experiences and identity formation. By centring this convergence of health, heritage, and habit, we see how diasporic practices are not only symbolic but somatic, imprinted onto bodies through repetitive, material routines, and embodied care.

Section 1.3 delves into the theoretical foundations that inform the analysis of objects as material agents in shaping social interactions and cultural identity. It examines how scholars have conceptualised materiality and objectification, particularly drawing on anthropological and sociological perspectives. To understand these dynamics, it is useful to briefly consider how materiality has been theorised in relation to human behaviour, social structures, and cultural practices.

1.3 Theoretical Foundations of Materiality and Objectification

Building on the discussion of how objects mediate social life, this section turns to the theoretical underpinnings that inform the study of materiality and objectification. It draws on anthropological, sociological, and philosophical frameworks to examine how objects participate in meaning-making, social reproduction, and identity formation. These theories provide the conceptual tools needed to analyse how material entities such as food, commodities, or shop layouts acquire symbolic value and shape discursive practices.

In 'Materiality: An Introduction', Daniel Miller (2005) critiques the insufficient anthropological study of objects and their relationship with materiality, calling for a deeper exploration of the role of 'things' in human lives. Miller draws on Erving Goffman's (1974) *Frame Analysis*, which explores how social interactions are structured by frames that guide behaviour, distinguishing between real and fabricated situations, and E. H. Gombrich's (1979) *The Sense of Order* which focuses on how frames, often unnoticed, elicit responses, particularly in art. He integrates these ideas into a broader theory of materiality, proposing that objects influence human behaviour in nuanced ways and contribute to the formation of material culture. Miller also draws on Pierre Bourdieu's (1977b) concept of 'practice', which emphasises habitual, unconscious actions embedded within social structures. For example, the arrangement of objects, like a dining table, reflects and reinforces social hierarchies. Such arrangements may index gender, class, and social roles, subtly directing embodied behaviour.

Miller delves further into objectification and explores the philosophical and theoretical challenges in defining 'things' and material culture. He critiques common-sense definitions and stresses the need for a broader philosophical framework. Drawing on Hegel's (1977) notion of objectification, where human creations acquire a life of their own and become alien to their creators (p. 8), he emphasises the dynamic interaction between human consciousness and material objects, challenging static views of materiality. A similar emphasis on a productive Hegelian subject–object relation appears in Noble (Noble, 2004), who highlights the centrality of objectification to self-formation and sociality, particularly within late-capitalist contexts of consumption. Both Miller and Noble stress the need to bring philosophical reflection into dialogue with ethnographic enquiry in order to better grasp the shifting nature of material culture.

Building on this foundational shift, scholarship in language and materiality (Cavanaugh & Shankar, 2014; Shankar & Cavanaugh, 2017) has emphasised the entanglement of linguistic and material processes, particularly in relation to how discourse both shapes and is shaped by materiality. For instance, food is not just a material substance but also a semiotic entity, deeply embedded in social and cultural practices (Cavanaugh & Shankar, 2014; Izadi, 2017). Language plays a crucial role in negotiating and transforming the meanings and values associated with food, as seen in marketising texts (Karrebæk & Maegaard, 2024) that construct imaginaries of places and culinary traditions. Such representations, as in the case of Persian shops and Persian food, do not merely describe but actively participate in shaping perceptions, desires, and social interactions. These processes illustrate how discourse does not simply reflect the world but co-constitutes it with material forms. The semiotic significance of food in these marketised spaces, therefore, becomes a dynamic force that influences how identities, class, and cultural values are articulated and consumed through both words and physical acts.

Extending this perspective, attending to the semiotic significance of food is crucial because it provides a site of engagement (Scollon, 2001), a moment in which material resources and social practices intersect to produce meaningful action, through which the entanglement of materiality, discourse, and identity becomes visible. In a similar vein, Noble (2002) reminds us that national identification is not only imagined or narrated but also materially and affectively experienced in the ordinary and familiar textures of daily life. The experience of 'homeliness' (p. 54), often evoked through objects, spaces, and embodied practices, anchors abstract categories like nationhood in mundane materialities, reinforcing ontological security and shaping subjectivity. As Miller (2005) argues, objects are not passive backdrops to social life but active participants in shaping practice and meaning. Food, as both a material and a semiotic object, xemplifies this dual role: it circulates within social fields structured by value, desire, and memory, while also being shaped by discursive framings that attach cultural and symbolic meanings to it (Shankar & Cavanaugh, 2017). In diasporic spaces, food not only indexes cultural belonging but also embodies the ongoing objectification of identity, where, following Hegel (1977), human meanings are projected onto things that then take on lives of their own. Focusing on food thus allows us to analyse how identities are not simply represented but materialised through socially and historically situated practices that involve both linguistic and non-linguistic resources.

1.4 Entanglements of Materiality and Language

The analysis of food as a material-semiotic object invites a broader theoretical reflection on the entangled nature of language and matter, a perspective central to recent new materialist approaches. Building on the previous discussion of materiality and objectification, we now turn to explore how these theoretical frameworks intersect with new materialist perspectives on language. Recent scholarship in new materialisms provides complementary insights into human-material relationships. Unlike the historical materialism of Marxism, which centres on economic relations, new materialisms emphasise the *entanglement* of the body with the material world, informed by feminist and phenomenological theories (Coole & Frost, 2010). These perspectives challenge *Enlightenment* notions of human exceptionalism and the passive treatment of nature as an instrumental resource. Bennett (2010) argues for the recognition of nonhuman materialities, such as electricity or fats, as active agents in shaping human experiences and actions. This reframing of agency positions objects and materials as integral actors in meaning-making and social dynamics rather than passive resources. Such a reorientation draws attention to nonhuman entities like food or objects as active forces shaping human behaviour and social structures. Karen Barad's (2003) concept of posthumanist performativity furthers this argument by questioning the boundaries between humans and nonhumans and examining the material-discursive practices that stabilise and destabilise these categories. In doing so, Barad (2003) challenges the Cartesian legacy and Saussurean structuralism (see also Lamb & Higgins, 2020), which have traditionally treated language and materiality as separate domains. By recognising these entanglements, we can move beyond the binary between language and materiality and explore how they interact in constituting social reality.

Extending Barad's (2003) focus on material-discursive practices, this theoretical understanding of language-material entanglements also extends to the materiality of language itself, which has been framed as 'an ontological move' (Shankar & Cavanaugh, 2017, p. 1), foregrounding how language possesses physical and metaphysical properties and is embedded within political-economic structures. Rather than treating language and materiality as separate, recent scholarship argues for understanding language as a material presence that has constitutive power. In this view, language is not only a tool for communication but also an embodied material practice that interacts with, and helps shape, broader societal forces. This perspective highlights how language, whether in the form of written texts, signage, or even embodied speech, is always already material, engaging with political, economic, and social structures in ways that exceed traditional representationalist views (Järlehed et al., 2023; Scollon & Scollon, 2003).

This resonates with Charles Peirce's triadic model of the sign, which treats meaning as an emergent relation among the material object, the sign itself, and its interpretant. Peirce's semiotic framework categorises signs into three interrelated components – icon, index, and symbol, depending on the nature of the sign's relation to its object. This triadic relation allows for meaning to arise not merely through symbolic abstraction but also through resemblance (iconicity) and existential contiguity (indexicality), grounding semiosis in both materiality and experience. Rather than reducing food discourse to a symbolic system, a Peircean perspective foregrounds the indexical and iconic dimensions of meaning-making, where the material presence of food (its smell, texture, or preparation) serves as a semiotic resource. Within this framework, Peirce also introduced the concept of 'qualisigns', that is, signs that convey meaning through qualities or sensations, such as a taste or smell, which are not necessarily propositional but felt. These qualisigns are closely related to what Peirce termed 'firstness', the category of pure feeling, possibility, and immediacy that precedes relational or conceptual mediation. In the context of food, such signs exemplify how material-affective sensations contribute to meaning in ways irreducible to language or representation. In this view, food functions as a dynamic assemblage of signs and sensations, embedded in cultural, affective, and political contexts.

This Peircean orientation to meaning as embodied and affective also resonates with broader arguments in linguistic anthropology and sociolinguistics that treat language itself as a material and socio-political phenomenon. As cited in Shankar and Cavanaugh (2017), William asserts that language requires physical forms while also functioning as a political-economic process reinforces this argument, suggesting that language should be understood not just as a vehicle of expression but as a constitutive force. This recognition is central to an expanded understanding of semiotic agency, where language emerges not only from the symbolic but also from the sensorial, political, and material conditions of its use. The recognition of language as a material entity offers a broader ontological lens through which we can understand how it shapes and is shaped by socio-political forces. As an active, embodied practice, language transcends simple representation, revealing itself as a tangible force that intertwines with power structures, shaping and being shaped by political, economic, and social conditions.

Connecting these ideas with more specific frameworks, this conceptualisation of language as both material and semiotic provides a bridge to the notion of semiofoodscapes (Järlehed & Moriarty, 2018, p. 26), where the interplay between discourse and materiality becomes especially evident. In this framework, food is not just a material object but a site where linguistic practices actively shape how food is experienced, appreciated, and understood. In doing so, semiofoodscapes bring to the forefront the multimodal and multisensorial dimensions of meaning-making, demonstrating how discourse and materiality are co-constitutive. Food thus becomes a critical intersection of language, materiality, and identity, where linguistic choices actively shape and are shaped by cultural perceptions and material experiences.

The intersection of language and materiality is clearly demonstrated in Elabdali's (2024) recent work on Arabic heritage language education in the United States. Here, cooking classes serve not merely as pedagogical tools but as emotionally charged, embodied practices of cultural belonging. Through cooking, students not only acquire vocabulary and syntax but also engage in what parents and teachers describe as 'living' cultural and linguistic experiences. The food practices documented in Elabdali's ethnographic study, such as making *manaeesh* or *kabees* (p. 65), are deeply embedded in everyday language use and foster affective attachments to heritage and identity. This account underscores how food mediates both linguistic learning and diasporic attachments, reinforcing the idea that semiofoodscapes are not neutral or decorative but emotionally and politically charged sites of meaning-making. These emotional and pedagogical dimensions further substantiate the semiotic-material frameworks outlined earlier, allowing for a more nuanced understanding of how food is mobilised to shape senses of belonging and continuity across generations and geographies.

Further research supports this entanglement of language, materiality, and affect. Language about food, for instance, does not simply describe taste; it plays a central role in shaping how food is perceived, valued, and consumed (Riley & Cavanaugh, 2017). Thurlow (2020) conceptualises food as a material, multimodal, and affective practice, where meaning arises through the interplay of discourse, embodiment, and sensory experience. In this way, food becomes a site where symbolic, affective, and material relations converge, demonstrating how language and materiality are inseparable in everyday life. These entanglements reveal that affect and sensation are not simply experienced but are mediated through semiotic and material forms. Rather than unfolding in isolation, meaning and agency emerge from shifting relations among bodies, objects, and discourses. Seen from this angle, language operates as a material force, integral to how we engage with and make sense of the world. This view also reframes material culture itself, showing how communicative and physical practices together mediate experience. Assemblages of people, things, and texts, then, do more than reflect social life; they actively participate in shaping cultural and economic realities (Pennycook, 2018a, 2018b).

1.5 Materiality and Agency in Deleuze and Guattari's Assemblages

Expanding on the earlier discussion of how objects and material forms actively shape human experiences and social practices, we now turn to a more specific conceptual framework, Deleuze and Guattari's (1987) notion of assemblages. This framework deepens our understanding of the agency of material forms by emphasising dynamic, fluid processes of association-making between humans, objects, and environments. It provides a lens through which we can explore how the unpredictable and relational nature of materiality intersects with human behaviour, power structures, and cultural meanings in lived, everyday contexts.

Their concept of assemblages reframes materiality as a field of flux and emergence, where humans, objects, and environments interact through non-linear, contingent relations. Their metaphors of rhizomes (decentralised networks) and trees (hierarchical structures) highlight the capacity of materiality to both resist and reinforce structural order, offering insights into how objects shape and are shaped by social forces. This perspective builds on earlier ideas about the active role of objects, adding dimensions of fluidity, unpredictability, and transformation to the discussion of materiality's agency. Connecting to these dynamics, Appadurai's (2015) concept of 'mediants' extends this view by showing that agency emerges not from discrete actors but from relations-in-motion. While Deleuze and Guattari (1987) focus on the unpredictable nature of assemblages, Appadurai foregrounds the intermediary quality of agentive formations. This relational view of materiality echoes Miller's (2005) work, where objects are seen not as passive entities but as active participants in shaping social dynamics. For example, in a marketplace, product displays not only convey information but also they mediate human behaviour and co-produce social meaning through an ongoing, emergent process.

Further advancing this concept, Caronia and Cooren's (2014) notion of 'ventriloquism' complements the assemblage perspective by proposing that objects, through their material presence, actively 'speak' and shape human action. This is clearly illustrated in examples such as queues, where objects 'call' humans into specific behaviours. This ventriloquistic view resonates with Deleuze and Guattari's (1987) assemblages by asserting that objects within a system are active, rather than passive, participants. Just as Appadurai describes how mediants shape the flow of social practices, ventriloquised objects like queues or product displays mediate human interactions and perform social functions. This is particularly relevant in the context of Persian shops in Sydney, where materiality is not merely functional but actively constructs cultural meaning. The placement of products, signage, and spatial arrangement (Izadi, 2015) becomes part of the assemblage that shapes the space, mediating cultural exchanges between Persian-speaking immigrants and non-Persian speakers. Here, materiality is affectively and semiotically charged; it carries social meaning that emerges through interaction, reinforcing cultural identities and shaping experiences. This is evident in the experience of a regular customer who feels 'reminded of home' not only by the products but also by the music playing in the shop and the aroma of loose tea and food. These sensory elements, along with the objects, evoke emotional resonance and act as cultural and affective agents, deepening identity and connection.

The emotional dimension of materiality is crucial for understanding how objects not only mediate social interaction but also serve as affective conduits for identity negotiation and cultural expression. In the context of migration, objects in spaces like shops can evoke memories of home, enhance feelings of belonging, and reinforce cultural identity (Izadi, 2017, 2020, 2023). In the case of Persian shops in Sydney, for example, the emotional resonance of products, scents, and sounds deepens customers' connection to their cultural heritage, creating a sense of continuity in a foreign environment. Objects in these spaces also become sites of cultural negotiation, particularly for immigrants navigating dual identities. Displays, images, and spatial arrangements mediate cultural differences and shared experiences. A regular customer may feel a sense of 'homecoming' not only through the products but also through the atmosphere created by these objects. This facilitates the negotiation of cultural identity, where the shop becomes a space in which customers actively (re)negotiate what it means to be Iranian/Persian, Australian, or both. Moreover, the emotional attachment to objects within these shops can foster emotional resilience, anchoring individuals in periods of cultural dislocation. These objects become more than material goods insofar as they take on affective significance and reinforce personal and collective identities. As Caronia and Cooren (2014) suggest, such objects are not merely mediators of consumer choice but agents in the emotional negotiation of belonging and cultural identity.

The role of material objects in shaping power dynamics in spaces like Persian shops goes beyond their function as mere facilitators of interaction. Objects, layouts, and product placements not only reflect existing power structures but actively participate in the creation and reinforcement of these structures. As part of the shop's assemblage, objects contribute to a polyphonic enactment of authority, where human and non-human actors combine to regulate behaviour and enforce social norms (Miller, 2005). The strategic arrangement of products such as luxury or culturally significant items establishes hierarchies of value, which signal what is culturally superior or desirable. This material organisation serves as a form of cultural governance, guiding customers' behaviours and reinforcing shared expectations about identity and belonging. At the same time, objects in these spaces can challenge and subvert traditional power dynamics, particularly when they serve to disrupt preconceived notions of cultural authenticity or authority. As Callon and Muniesa (2005) argue, the material world is not a passive backdrop but an active participant in shaping social relations, where objects mediate power and represent ongoing negotiations of identity and authority.

In Sections 1–5, we explored various theoretical frameworks to understand the relationship between materiality, language, and agency. Beginning with how materiality shapes human experience, we expanded on the role of language in mediating material interactions. We also integrated Latour's view of agency and actants, alongside the concepts of Deleuze and Guattari's (1987) assemblages, Appadurai's 'mediants' and Caronia and Cooren's 'ventriloquism'. Together, these perspectives refine our understanding of materiality as an active, relational force that influences human behaviour, social interactions, and cultural meanings, particularly in spaces such as Persian shops in Sydney. Having established these foundational ideas, the next section outlines the ethnographic methodology used to observe and analyse material interactions in these spaces.

2 Methodology and Analytical Tools

This section outlines the methodology and analytical tools used in the study. The primary framework, Linguistic Ethnography (LE), offers a detailed analysis of how language and communication practices are embedded within broader social and cultural contexts (Rampton, 2007). By combining ethnographic methods with discourse-analytic techniques, LE provides a comprehensive approach to understanding how meaning is constructed through interactions, institutional settings, and material objects. In addition, MDA is used to explore how material objects, such as traditional textiles in a Persian shop, act as mediational tools influencing social relations and practices. Together, LE and MDA offer an integrated perspective on the dynamic relationships between discourse, materiality, and agency. To operationalise these frameworks, ethnographic field notes were written immediately after each visit, capturing both verbal exchanges and contextual elements such as spatial arrangements, customer movement, and the placement and handling of material objects. Audio recordings of interactions were made using two unobtrusive digital devices and selectively transcribed using a combination of orthographic and simplified conversation-analytic conventions, with attention to pauses, overlaps, and prosodic features. Where Persian was spoken, the transcripts were translated into English, with careful attention to preserving pragmatic and cultural nuance. These transcripts were then thematically coded in conjunction with field notes, allowing for a triangulated analysis of participants' talk, embodied practices, and their spatial-material context (see Izadi, 2020).

Although the data were collected between 2012 and 2014, the delay in reporting stems from the evolving nature of the theoretical and analytical frameworks used. Over the past decade, I have been refining my approach, particularly in relation to the integration of Linguistic Ethnography and Mediated Discourse Analysis and drawing on recent theoretical advancements in materiality and semiotics. This longitudinal engagement with the data has allowed for a more nuanced and conceptually robust analysis. Importantly, the themes explored such as diaspora, identity, language, and the role of material objects remain deeply relevant to current sociolinguistic and anthropological debates, particularly in multicultural and diasporic contexts like Australia. Rather than being outdated, the data provide a historically situated lens through which to understand enduring and still-evolving dynamics of belonging, agency, and cultural transmission.

Data were collected from interactions observed in a Persian shop in Sydney over a five-year period. This approach enables an examination of how agency is enacted in various social practices. Data collection occurred through over ninety visits between October 2012 and October 2014, with two strategically placed digital audio-recording devices capturing diverse interactions between shop-owners and customers. These recordings allowed for the analysis of both the interactions and the role of material objects, such as products imported from Iran, in shaping agency in these social settings. Qualitative analysis, including thematic coding and nexus analysis of recorded interactions and field notes, helped identify patterns of agency exhibited by both objects and individuals. By examining micro-interactions, the study reveals how material objects contribute to identity formation and engage with broader social meanings, such as cultural identity and health narratives.

In conducting this ethnographic study, I was acutely aware of my own positionality and the complex, often shifting roles I inhabited within the Persian shop. Drawing on Duranti's (1997, p. 99) distinction between passive and complete participant-observation, my approach moved fluidly between both modes. At times I sat back to observe interactions with minimal interference; at other moments, particularly in quieter times or with familiar customers, I actively engaged in conversations, asked questions, or reflected with the shop-owner after interactions. This hybrid role (researcher, participant, and at times perceived assistant) was not only strategic but necessary in building trust and accessing the deeper socio-cultural dynamics at play (Agar, 1997). These fluid transitions helped surface the vernacular routines, speech practices, and informal literacies of everyday life in the shop, which may otherwise have gone unnoticed. Over time, my presence became normalised, allowing me to witness not just scripted exchanges but the subtle negotiations of identity, humour, and belonging that occurred in and around transactions.

Far from being a neutral observer, I was implicated in the field through my social ties with the shop-owners and the broader community. My familiarity with the setting and my visible, ongoing presence shaped how I was perceived: sometimes as an insider, sometimes as a researcher, and occasionally as an ambiguous presence that prompted hesitation or discomfort, particularly when participants noticed the recording signs. These moments underscored the ethical complexities of fieldwork and reminded me that full detachment was neither feasible nor desirable. Rather than claiming objective neutrality, I adopted a reflexive stance, critically assessing how my own assumptions, emotions, and positionality affected data collection and interpretation (Norris, 2011, p. 73). This was especially important during politically sensitive conversations, where my silence was often a methodological choice to avoid influencing the flow of interaction. In such moments, awareness of my performative role enabled a form of ethical responsiveness that prioritised participant comfort and consent. Ultimately, I came to understand my role not as fixed but as performative and negotiated, shifting depending on context, participants, and the social rhythms of the shop. While I was not a full member of the community, my long-standing relationship with the shop-owners and prior experience in Persian commercial spaces afforded me a level of trust and access that enriched the data. This relational grounding, coupled with analytical distance, enabled me to observe how social identities and material practices intersect in diasporic commercial life, while also navigating the personal, political, and epistemological stakes of fieldwork in familiar terrain. At times, this meant working against my own instincts or suppressing disagreement to preserve the ethnographic moment. Yet it was precisely this tension, between proximity and distance, familiarity and estrangement, that sharpened my critical lens and deepened the interpretive value of the study.

The analysis also integrates interactional sociolinguistics, which conceptualises 'conversational inference' (Gumperz, 2015, p. 313) as interactively achieved through diverse semiotic repertoires across expansive spatiotemporal contexts. This approach expands the analytical focus beyond face-to-face interactions, incorporating a broader view of how meaning is constructed. Gumperz's construction of 'repertoire' extends beyond singularly labelled languages to encompass a variety of semiotic resources. He defines repertoire as encompassing 'all the accepted ways of formulating messages' (Gumperz, 1964, pp. 137–138) and describes it as 'the totality of linguistic forms regularly employed within the community in the course of socially significant interaction' (Gumperz, 1971, p. 182). Sociolinguists have since expanded this to include various communicative methods more than just 'linguistic forms'. Rymes (2010, p. 528) introduces the notion of 'communicative repertoire', which includes 'the collection of ways individuals use language and literacy and other means of communication (gestures, dress, posture, or accessories) to function effectively in the multiple communities in which they participate'. Building on this, Blommaert and Backus (2013, p. 25; Bucholtz & Hall, 2016) argue that 'a repertoire is composed of a myriad of different communicative tools, with different degrees of functional specialisation. No single resource is a communicative panacea; none is useless'. These expanded notions of semiotic resources offer a richer understanding of objects and their capacity for meaning-making.

In addition, the analysis draws on the concept of small stories (De Fina & Georgakopoulou, 2015), which refers to fragmented, often co-constructed narratives that arise in everyday conversation. Unlike traditional, high-stakes narratives, small stories emerge spontaneously in informal contexts and are crucial to how participants position themselves, claim knowledge, and negotiate belonging. This lens is particularly productive in diasporic commercial spaces, where customers and shop-owners frequently engage in storytelling about food, memory, or migration that indexes broader identity processes (Izadi, 2020). Attention to these narrative moments enriches the analysis of agency and cultural transmission by capturing how social meaning is collaboratively assembled in interaction.

Drawing from these theoretical foundations, the next section explores how material objects function as agents in meaning-making. By analysing their semiotic and social roles, we gain deeper insight into how language, materiality, and agency shape agency and cultural identity within Persian commercial spaces.

Discourse, Materiality & Agency within Everyday Social Interactions 23

3 Objects as Mediators in the Semiotic Landscape

This section begins with an analysis of two different Persian shop signs: one displaying the phrase '100% Halal' (Figure 1) and the other featuring the Faravahar symbol (Figure 2), an ancient emblem of the Zoroastrian faith. The Faravahar, depicting a bearded man with an outstretched hand above wings emanating from a circle that symbolises eternity, carries profound cultural and historical significance. As cultural artefacts, both signs serve as material representations of specific beliefs and practices, deeply rooted in the cultural landscapes of their respective communities. Importantly, these signs are part of

Figure 1 The 100% Halal sign as an actant

Figure 2 The Faravahar symbol as an actant

a larger semiotic landscape (Jaworski & Thurlow, 2010) that surrounds and informs the shop environment, embedding individual signs within a broader field of linguistic, symbolic, and cultural resources that collectively construct the identity of the place and its community. This semiotic landscape shapes how these signs are interpreted and how they function socially, as they contribute to the ongoing discourse within Persian commercial and diasporic settings. The signs therefore do not only point to fixed religious or cultural identities but rather participate in the negotiation of such identities within a fluid and dynamic communicative environment. This perspective offers a broader lens for examining how material objects such as shop signs function as semiotic resources that shape and reflect cultural identities within Persian commercial spaces. The presence of the '100% Halal' sign materialises moral and religious orientations in the shop, shaping normative expectations and signalling a particular ethical terrain to customers. Similarly, the Faravahar symbol mediates collective memory and spiritual identity, thus enrolling the shop environment in broader moral-political assemblages.

If we conceptualise the '100% Halal' sign and the Faravahar symbol as instances of mediational tools and 'frozen action' (Norris, 2004), which refers to actions carried out by social actors at an earlier time and preserved for future interactions, then these signs might correspond to what Latour (2005) refers to as 'intermediaries'. Latour (2005) distinguishes between 'intermediaries', which pass meaning unchanged, and 'mediators', which transform or modify the meaning as it passes through them. In this case, while the signs originate from social actors, their presence actively reshapes meanings and social relations in the shop context, thus acting as mediators rather than passive intermediaries. Drawing on Latour's (2005) framework of actants and Cooren's (2004) notion of 'textual agency', these signs actively shape behaviours and embed cultural meanings, functioning as mediators that influence the social fabric of their contexts. As mediators, these signs do not simply transmit pre-existing meanings; rather, they participate in the transformation and circulation of meaning in relation to both context and audience. In this sense, they can be seen as actively participating (hybrid actants, Latour, 1993) in the social and cultural practices they represent, steering interactions by orienting them towards specific cultural values or religious principles.

This agency is inseparable from the semiotic landscape in which these signs are situated: they do not operate in isolation but interact dynamically with other signs, texts, and cultural markers visible in the environment, collectively constructing a social space that is culturally and ideologically meaningful. This dynamic of mediation highlights their role in shaping the actions and perceptions (Lou, 2016) of individuals and extends beyond simple representation to position them as agents in the social landscape.

Building on this conceptualisation, we can further examine their status as 'objects'. If we define 'objects' as tangible or intangible entities (Izadi & Luke, 2025) that are capable of action or are attributed with agency (Cerulo, 2009, 2011), it becomes evident that these signs qualify as such. Here, the term 'object' extends beyond physical entities to encompass non-human 'things', such as symbols, signs, and cultural artefacts. Drawing on Cooren's (2010) philosophical notion of 'objects', which encompasses non-human figures or characters that carry meaning and exert influence, these signs emerge as distinct types of 'things'. For instance, the '100% Halal' sign actively fosters a sense of trust and religious alignment among customers, while the Faravahar (Figure 2) evokes cultural identity and historical continuity. The materiality of the '100% Halal' sign shapes social behaviours by aligning individuals with moral and religious codes. It not only functions as a symbol of religious correctness but also mediates social cohesion within Muslim communities, reinforcing class distinctions and in-group identities. Their role as objects is further amplified by their embeddedness in the semiotic landscape, where their presence alongside other signs contributes to a multilayered environment of meaning-making that resonates with viewers and customers on multiple levels – religious, cultural, social, and commercial.

As non-human agents, these signs embody indexicality, which references specific cultural or religious contexts through their mere presence (Silverstein, 2003). They also function as qualisigns in Peirce's (1995) semiotics, representing qualities or characteristics that evoke emotions such as trust or cultural pride, which resonate with viewers. The '100% Halal' sign, for example, indexes both religious correctness and the moral alignment of the restaurant with Muslim dietary laws, while the Faravahar sign invokes the cultural and historical continuity of Zoroastrianism, indexing a specific identity tied to its community. These indexical signs exemplify Peirce's idea of *firstness*, where the sign stands as a potential quality, inviting interpretation without determining a definitive meaning. As objects, these signs, though static, continuously engage with their viewers, offering interpretations that shape social interactions and cultural identities. In this way, they transcend being mere identity markers and instead mediate and reinforce cultural and social norms, simultaneously illustrating the dynamic interplay between cultural artefacts and social agency. This interpretative openness contributes to their affective force, allowing viewers to attribute personal and communal meanings to the signs and engage with them on a visceral level. The semiotic landscape thus functions as a contextual frame, allowing these signs to be read not only as isolated objects but as part of a network of signs that collectively produce social meaning and identity in the Persian diasporic space.

Similarly, the Faravahar symbol (Figure 2) functions as a cultural agent deeply embedded in the temporal and spatial dimensions of Zoroastrian heritage and broader Iranian identity. Its placement on the shop sign transcends mere decoration; it actively fosters a connection to ancient Persia and its cultural landscapes, evoking a sense of authenticity and historical value (Pietikäinen et al., 2016). This connection situates the symbol within a broader temporal framework, where it embodies the enduring values and philosophies of Zoroastrianism, such as the triad of 'Good Thoughts, Good Words, and Good Deeds'. These principles are not abstract ideals but are integrated into the daily practices of the shop-owner, as evidenced by their customer interactions and ethical business practices. Notably, the symbol mediates interactions in unexpected ways, as observed when non-Persian-speaking customers enquire about its meaning. This curiosity transforms the Faravahar symbol into an active participant in cross-cultural dialogue, linking the materiality of the symbol with its social and cultural significance. Through these exchanges, the owner explains its historical and religious significance, creating a space where the symbol bridges cultural gaps and facilitates an understanding of Zoroastrian philosophy. In this way, the symbol also evokes nostalgia, calling on a shared history and cultural continuity that resonates with both the owner and customers. This relational function positions the Faravahar not only as a site of memory but as a prompt for narrative exchange, a node around which stories of identity and belonging are shared and reconstructed.

Here, we observe the 'thingness' (Heidegger, 1935 in Saurma-Jeltsch, 2010) of the Faravahar, not merely as a physical artefact but as an entity embedded in a specific cultural, temporal, and spatial landscape, with its own agency. Crucially, this embedding situates the Faravahar within the Persian semiotic landscape of the shop's locale, where it converses with other cultural signs, linguistic markers, and the broader environment, thus participating in the production of a culturally rich semiotic field that is meaningful for both insiders and outsiders.

From an ontological perspective, the Faravahar embodies what Henare et al. (2007) view as a holistic understanding of 'thingness', where objects are not just connected to human societies but are deeply intertwined with local places, specific times, and unique cultural landscapes. This situatedness allows the symbol to transcend static objecthood and emerge as a 'mediator' of cultural practices, historical continuity, and moral values. Its presence evokes what Bourdieu (1985) might consider an act of distinction: the symbol asserts a unique cultural identity, setting the shop apart and embedding it within a rich cultural narrative that resists commodification (see also Jaworski,

2015). The Faravahar also exemplifies the 'power of resistance' as its enduring presence resists erasure or dilution in the face of contemporary socio-political dynamics. Under Iran's current regime, its presence may signify subtle resistance, a quiet assertion of cultural heritage and identity that challenges dominant discourses. This symbolic resistance amplifies the Faravahar's role as an actant, actively shaping perceptions and reinforcing a sense of historical and cultural continuity in a modern diasporic setting.

In sum, the Faravahar and the '100% Halal' sign are not merely markers of identity but are actants that mediate and sustain the interplay between materiality, morality, and cultural identity. Their agency lies in their ability to embed cultural norms, facilitate social interactions, and preserve moral codes, illustrating how objects dynamically participate in shaping the cultural and social fabric. Through these interactions, the Faravahar symbolises the intersection of cultural heritage, resistance, and social meaning. For diasporic communities, the Faravahar may be seen as an emblem of resistance to cultural assimilation (Izadi & Parvaresh, 2016), while local Iranians may interpret it as a symbol of national pride or cultural continuity, in contrast to the government's view of it as a contested symbol of pre-revolutionary identity. The Faravahar, in particular, exemplifies the ontological turn by embodying both its material and cultural essence, firmly anchored in time, place, and the landscapes of Zoroastrian heritage. Through its interaction with customers and its power to evoke curiosity and distinction, it highlights the interconnectedness of objects, agency, and social worlds, ultimately affirming its role as a vital contributor to cultural production and social meaning. This shift in focus allows us to explore how signs function not only as semiotic markers but also as active participants in the interaction. Integrating the concept of the semiotic landscape throughout this analysis underscores how these signs operate not only as individual markers but as components of a wider cultural and linguistic environment that shapes and is shaped by their presence and agency.

4 Material Objects and Institutional Agency in Practice

In contrast to the previous discussion of symbolic acts in cultural contexts, the following section turns to Extract 1, which takes place within a Persian shop, to highlight the mediating role of material objects in everyday social exchanges. While the Faravahar and the '100% Halal' sign serve as cultural symbols, this extract shifts attention to another object – the recording sign – which plays a key role in governing behaviour, ensuring ethical practices, and influencing social dynamics. This orientation is initially prompted by a sign indicating that recording is in progress, which becomes a catalyst for the interaction that follows. To clarify from the outset, the recording device itself, along with the sign, will be analysed not only as a technical tool but as a material object whose presence is socially and ethically consequential. The interaction illustrates how the recording device enters the participants' shared attention, influences their behaviour, and structures the discourse through its institutional and ethical affordances. This example demonstrates how such objects function beyond mere representation, carrying both symbolic and institutional meanings.

A brief reflection on contradictory agencies of material objects, for example, the Halal sign unifying Muslims while simultaneously delineating religious boundaries, can further enrich this analysis. In this regard, the Halal sign not only affirms shared values among Muslim customers but also introduces a boundary that distinguishes them from others, demonstrating how the same object can simultaneously include and exclude. Through the lens of Extract 1, we can observe how objects carry not just symbolic meanings but also institutional and legal functions that shape human behaviour.

Extract 1

OB: Older brother: A Persian-speaking customer in his mid-40s who grew up in Sydney
C2: Younger brother: A Persian-speaking customer in his mid-20s, born in Australia to Persian parents
SOW: The shop-owner, the wife
SOH: The Shop-owner, the husband
Text Format: Persian text is in `Courier New`, while translations are in Times New Roman.
Researcher's Comments: Comments are enclosed in double parentheses ((...)).

1	OB	`You know we've got a recorder here. He ((the researcher)) told us earlier.` `Look at that sign. You're being recorded here. He ((the researcher)) told us`
2	YB	`why?`
3	OB	`he's doing he's doing research`
4	YB	`why's he recording us?`
5	OB	`here's the sign he told us`
6	YB	`why's he recording us?`
7	OB	`just ((laughing)) don't swear ((laughing)) don't swear`
8	YB	`what's he recording?`
9	OB	`voice ((everyone laughing))`
10	YB	`Why?`
11	SOW	`laughing`
12	YB	`is there a camera?`
13	OB	`no just the voice ((shop-owners laughing))`
14	YB	`where's the voice?`

15	SOW	laughing and saying where's the voice?
16	YB	how did I miss this sign? ((everyone's laughing now)) ((he's reading the sign now)) Intercultural communication OK
17	OB	did you get the ice cream or not ((Everyone's laughing now))
18	YB	everybody, calm down. We have a cultural... we're breaking ((inaudible))barriers between Persians and Persians. ((Now C1 to C2 while speaking in Persian))
19	OB to YB:	بستنی رو گرفتی؟ did you get the ice-cream?
20	OB:	بستنی نمی خوام بسته کشتی ما رو. I don't want ice cream. You've killed me ((C2 is annoyed as C1 keeps asking if he needs ice cream))
21	SOW	don't pay for it just free
22	YB	no no I can't are you saying it because it's recorded and you wanna look good? ((Everyone is laughing now))
22	OB	C1 turning to me before saying goodbye, speaking in Persian)) ((If anything comes out of it, let me know)) . اگه چیزی دراومدازش بهم خبر بده

In this interaction, a family visits a Persian shop where I collected my data. The group consists of an older brother (OB), a younger brother (YB), and the shop-owners (SOW and SOH). The shop-owners are a Persian-Australian couple who, at the time of data collection, had been running the store for approximately ten years and continue to operate it today. Having migrated to Australia over four decades ago, they are long-term residents who identify strongly with both their Persian heritage and their Australian context. Persian is their first language and the main language used in private and behind-the-counter conversations, while English is used fluently and regularly in customer interactions. Their bilingual repertoire and bicultural positioning shape the linguistic environment of the shop, influencing not only their communicative practices but also the broader semiotic and cultural landscape in which the interaction unfolds.

Extract 1 occurs at the counter where the family is about to pay. Throughout the interaction, the older brother repeatedly suggests that the younger brother try ice cream, but the younger brother resists. As part of the exchange, the older brother (in line 1) draws attention to a sign on the counter, stating, 'You know we've got a recorder here. He ((the researcher)) told us earlier. Look at that sign. You're being recorded here. He ((the researcher)) told us.' The sign, prominently displayed at the counter, reads: '*Your interaction is being recorded. If you don't want your interaction to be recorded, please let the researcher or the shop-owners know.*' The reference to the sign introduces a new dynamic into the interaction, as it shifts the participants' focus to the ongoing recording and its implications. This sign can be analysed as a 'mediational means' (Scollon, 2001), as it functions as a material object that shapes and mediates the interaction. Its agency lies not in its physical presence alone but in how it is imbued with institutional meanings and norms. The sign represents more than a simple mechanism for attracting participants' attention and securing their consent. It symbolises the culmination of a rigorous process, as it took the researcher four to five months to obtain ethics approval from the university before being allowed to record interactions. This approval process involved meeting strict legal and ethical standards, underscoring the sign's role as a legal document embedded within broader institutional frameworks. As such, the sign embodies the intersection of research ethics, institutional oversight, and the researcher's accountability, making it an actant that structures and governs the interaction in significant ways. Thus, the presence of the sign and the wording dictate certain actions and expectations, such as notifying the researcher or shop-owners if a customer does not wish to be recorded. This indicates the objectified role of the sign within this specific socio-cultural and institutional context. The illocutionary force of the sign (Austin, 1962) operates as a reminder to customers and highlights the recording process while maintaining an ethical safeguard. It does not merely display information but actively engages the participants, urging them to act or respond based on its content. The location of the sign on the counter, where transactions occur, further emphasises its agency and makes it central to the interaction.

The role of the sign can be further understood through the theoretical lenses of Latour (1996a, 1996b, 2005), Appadurai (2015), and Scollon (2001). From Latour's (2005) perspective, the sign can be understood as an actant, as it participates in the network of interactions, influencing and organising the behaviour of the participants. Its materiality and positioning afford it the power to shape the discourse and remind the customers of the normative framework established by the ethics committee and the researcher's presence. Similarly, in light of Appadurai's (2015) concept of the mediant, the sign serves as a node (Zhu et al., 2017) where different forces and contexts converge. It connects the local context of the shop with broader institutional and ethical frameworks, enabling the participants to navigate their roles within this mediated space. The sign's capacity to 'do things without words', that is, 'its performative force' (Caron & Caronia, 2007, p. 36), is evident in how it prompts questions, laughter, and reflection among the participants, as seen in lines 2–16. Ultimately, the meaning of the sign and its agency are not static but emerge dynamically through its interaction with people, objects, and contexts. The interplay of the participants' responses and the sign's presence illustrates how material objects can embody and enforce social norms, which demonstrates their active role in shaping discourse and action.

Apart from the sign, two other objects in Extract 1 stand out in shaping the discourse: the ice cream and the recording device. Both objects play active roles in mediating the interaction, influencing the customers' behaviour, and structuring the interaction in ways that are culturally and ethically significant. The ice cream is more than a simple consumable item in this interaction; it becomes a point of negotiation and social interaction between the older brother and the younger brother. OB repeatedly encourages YB to try the ice cream, but YB resists. This repeated focus on the ice cream introduces an element of agency for both customers. OB's insistence is a form of social influence, which subtly guides the conversation towards the ice cream as a social object. YB's resistance, in turn, reflects his autonomy, as he pushes back against OB's suggestion and asserts control over his own choices. In this sense, the ice cream functions as a mediator of social roles, revealing the dynamics between the two brothers, OB takes on a more dominant role by persistently suggesting the ice cream, while YB resists, asserting his personal agency. Moreover, the ice cream serves as a distraction from the more formal, institutional aspects of the interaction, such as the ethical implications of the recording. As the conversation shifts toward humour and light-heartedness about the ice cream, the tension created by the presence of the recording device is temporarily diffused. This light-hearted focus on the ice cream allows the participants to interact more casually, while the underlying ethical structure remains implicit in the background. This illustrates how objects, like the ice cream, are not passive but can actively shape the flow of interaction by providing a means of distraction or relief from more serious topics.

The recording device also plays a central role in structuring the ethical and institutional framework of the interaction. Unlike the ice cream, which facilitates social bonding and negotiation, the recording device introduces a layer of formality and accountability to the exchange. The device, by enabling the documentation of the conversation, makes the participants aware of being observed. In line 22, when YB questions the shop-owner, asking, 'Are you saying it because it's recorded and you wanna look good?' the recording device is directly implicated in the interaction. Here, the device is not just a passive tool for capturing data but an actant that shapes social norms and influences behaviour through its embedded ethical and institutional functions.

From Latour's (2005) perspective, both the ice cream and the recording device are actants within a network of interactions, each influencing the customers' behaviour and the flow of the interaction. The ice cream functions as an object that mediates social dynamics, while the recording device acts as an object that enforces institutional norms. Together, these objects highlight how material things, whether mundane or institutional, carry the performative force to shape discourse, action, and interaction.

The transition between Extract 1 and Extract 2 marks a distinct shift in both physical and discursive context, where the focus moves from object influence to the centrality of tobacco as a subject of discourse. Extract 2 takes place at the entrance near the cash register where the tobacco is positioned. SW is standing behind the cash register. The interaction order is in small 'withs' (Scollon & Scollon, 2004), an event in which two or more people are seen as being together with one another and having their focus on their own interaction (see also Izadi, 2015, 2017), on the border of formal and informal whose participants have relatively equal status in their right to hold the floor, and the topic of conversation is 'tobacco'. However, their historical bodies (Scollon & Scollon, 2004) (their habitus) may be significantly different because the shop-owner is perhaps viewed as the connoisseur of the items of the shop and of Persian values, with knowledge about a particular product (mediational means) that requires knowledge of the standard variety. The participants in this interaction speak English.

> ((I'm talking to SW about a customer who has just left the shop. Suddenly, a new customer comes in and we stop talking. English music is on and it's loud enough. SW is cleaning the counter and takes a short look at the entrance and suddenly sees C).)

Extract 2

C: The customer
SOW: shop-owner (the wife)

1	C	you know what if I give you this card rather (.) that's my husband's sees the smoke on this card bill hhh he doesn't like me smoking ...
2	SOW	it's a [credit
3	C	[yeah
4	SOW	and signature (.) or pin (.) or]
5	C	yeah (.)sign (1.0) he says I smoke <u>too much</u>
6	SOW	(2 sec) ((looking down no eye contact))

While paying at the counter, the customer has already given the shop-owner her husband's credit card and suddenly changes her mind, asking the shop-owner whether she could use her own instead in line 1: 'that's my husband's sees the smoke on this card bill hhh', followed by a laugh. Here, from an MDA perspective, the husband's credit card has become an important mediational means. Following Latour's ANT, the credit card is not merely an object but an actant, shaping the interaction and mediating the relationship between the absent husband, the customer, and the shop-owner. Even though the husband is not present, he is brought into play as part of a distributed agency where the material artefact (the card) acts as an extension of his surveillance and authority. The customer provides an account of why she cannot use her husband's credit card: 'He doesn't like me smoking' (line 1), situating the card as an 'inscription device' (Latour & Woolgar, 1986) that carries and enforces moral and social constraints beyond the immediate transaction.

In Extract 2, we can observe a prime example of an actant at work. The credit card is not merely a passive object facilitating transactions; it is an active participant in shaping social dynamics and relationships. It exerts agency by mediating power relations, influencing the customer's behaviour, and invoking the absent husband's authority. Building on Miller's (2005) perspective on materiality, the credit card is not simply an economic tool, but a material object embedded in broader socio-moral structures, reinforcing gendered expectations, financial control, and moral surveillance. Here, the card enables a purchase. It materialises an external authority, which shapes the interaction and positions the customer in a moment of moral and financial negotiation. From an MDA (Scollon, 2001) perspective, the credit card serves as a historically shaped mediational tool, which carries with it a sedimented history of social norms and financial governance. The participants at this site of engagement have different relationships with this actant – while the shop-owner engages with it as a functional tool within the commercial setting, the customer encounters it as a symbol of constraint, which creates a tension between personal autonomy and spousal oversight. These intersecting networks of practice (Latour, 2005) expose the entanglement of materiality, discourse, and agency, illustrating how seemingly mundane objects actively structure human interactions and moral negotiations.

Furthermore, it seems that on account of the credit card as an actant and mediational tool in this interaction, the backstage activities may have become frontstage ones. Originating from Goffman (1959), the twin notions of 'frontstage' and 'backstage' suggest that individuals in their daily dealings have two different modes of presenting themselves to others, namely one when they are 'on the stage' (frontstage) and the other when they let down their guard (backstage), which is 'out of bounds to members of the audience' (p.79). Here, the credit card as an actant not only mediates but actively restructures the interactional script, pulling the customer's private concerns (her smoking habits, marital surveillance) into the public arena of the shop. This shift highlights how the materiality of the card brings backstage concerns into the frontstage, making private matters visible in the public sphere of the transaction. In doing so, it functions as a non-human participant, which reinforces the performative nature of social order and shifts the boundaries between personal autonomy and institutionalised control.

The frontstage activities now necessitate different rules of the game (see Blommaert & De Fina, 2017) that change completely while the new rule of the game simultaneously displays different identities of the participants present in the discourse at hand and, more importantly, those who are not present (the husband, for instance), that arise from the 'intertextual' (Blommaert, 2005; Silverstein, 2003) relations between the mediational means and the linguistic utterances produced by the participants. The interaction order, therefore, is not simply defined by immediate co-presence but by the distributed agency of absent others, mediated by the credit card as a technological and semiotic device. For instance, at the start of the sequence (line 1), the customer accomplishes the action of displaying concern that she does not wish her husband to find out that she is smoking. This creates a moment of friction between competing actants within a network: the husband's surveillance, the customer's autonomy, and the shop-owner's professional role, all intersecting with moral positioning.

After the customer has stated her problem and entered the frontstage (i.e., not allowed to smoke), it would be expected to be followed by compliance on the part of the shop-owner. Nonetheless, in line 2, after a pause of two seconds, her account is not taken up by the shop-owner. The shop-owner then directly goes to the business and asks whether it is a credit card, a signature, or a pin in line 4. This disalignment could be seen as a moment where competing actants and mediational means shape the trajectory of interaction: the customer seeks affective alignment through self-disclosure, while the shop-owner adheres to the transactional frame imposed by the material and discursive agency of the credit card. The card, as an actant, enforces a shift back to the commercial logic of the transaction, resisting the emotional framing attempted by the customer. It seems that the shop-owner is fulfilling the category-bound 'duties' (Sacks, 1992) of expressing concern here as a (responsible) moral actor within a network in which both human and non-human actants interact to structure the discourse.

Due to the routine nature of the service interactions at least in the shop in question, expectations about the roles and identities are rather fixed. Accordingly, deviation from the pre-established roles may give rise to negative potential imputations of identities that produce negative consequences for the deviant customer, for example, a disobedient wife. Through the lens of ANT, the shop is not merely a backdrop but an active node (Zhu et al., 2017) in a network of human and non-human actants, shaping the moral and transactional landscape. The credit card, as an actant, operates within this network to link economic exchanges with social discipline, which reinforces gendered norms and financial surveillance. In this sense, the material environment, comprising

Discourse, Materiality & Agency within Everyday Social Interactions

the shop, the card, and the customer's relational ties, becomes an assemblage through which power and social order are enacted.

Building on the interplay of objects and agency in Extract 2, Extract 3 shifts focus to another scenario in which documents, specifically a power of attorney, become pivotal in mediating social and transactional relations. This interaction begins with a customer who frequently visits the shop, engaging the shop-owners in a discussion about the sale of land in northern Iran, bringing the concept of delegation and legal documentation to the forefront.

Extract 3

C: A Persian-speaking customer in his mid-40s
SOW: The shop-owner, the wife
SOH: The Shop-owner, the husband
Researcher's Comments: Comments are enclosed in double parentheses ((...)).

1 SOW   یه زمینی تو شمال کلاردشت داریم می خواستیم بفروشیمش از بابام خواستیم این کار و برامون انجام بده.
We own a piece of land in northern Iran, in Kelardasht, ((a popular tourist place in Mazandaran province)) that we're planning to sell. I've asked my dad to handle the sale for us.

2 C   خوب شما باید وکالت بدین که براتون این کارو انجام بدن. میدونم داره بنگاه دادشم از چون.
Well, you'll need to give him power of attorney to legally manage the process for you. I know how it works because my brother owns an agency ((meaning he is a realtor)).

3 SOW   بله خودمون می دونیم، هر کاری که لازم باشه انجام می دیم.
Yes, we know. We'll do whatever is necessary.

4 C   کجای کلاردشته؟
Where in Kelardasht is it?

6 SOH   بالا، قسمت روستای عباس آباده.
Up in the Abbas Abad village area.

7 C   ما هم ویلا داریم، اسب چین، بعد از متل قو سمت شهسوار.
We have a villa too, in Asb Chin, past Motel Ghoo ((name of a famous hotel near Kelardasht)), towards Tonekabon ((a city in Mazandaran Province near Kelardasht)).

8 SO   ما وکالت می دیم.
We'll give the power of attorney.

9 C   چون متراژش کمه زود به فروش می ره.
Since the size ((of the land)) is small, it will sell quickly.

10 SO   دورش دیوار هم کشیدیم.
We've also fenced it.

11 C   خوب این خیلی تو فروشش تأثیر داره رو هوا می برنش. خوب من در موردش حتماً صحبت می کنم.
That's great! It will have a big impact on the sale – people will snap it up in no time. I'll definitely discuss this with my brother.

12 SOH   خیلی ممنون
Thanks very much

In Extract 3, a customer who regularly visits the shop while paying at the counter engages the shop-owners in a conversation about a piece of land he owns in northern Iran, in the Mazandaran province. The shop-owner (the wife) mentions she also has land in that region, and the customer notes that, since they are based in Australia, they cannot personally sell it. Instead, they would need to grant a power of attorney to someone in Iran to take care of the sale (line 2). The shop-owner (the husband) acknowledges this with certainty (line 3). At this juncture, the conversation highlights the role of objects and documents as actants in the exchange. Specifically, the power of attorney acts as a material entity that mediates the human interaction by enabling the transfer of responsibility. In line with Latour's (1996b) view, the act of delegation is not merely a human action but involves a network of actants, where the document itself becomes part of the action. The power of attorney, as a material object, not only facilitates the delegation of responsibility but also acts as an enabler of agency, moving beyond the human actors to mediate the transaction in a meaningful way. Here, Latour's concept of actants helps to underscore how human agency is intertwined with non-human objects (such as documents), forming a hybrid network where both contribute to the outcome.

Importantly, this interaction also invites us to consider the agency of immaterial-semiotic forms such as the concept of legal delegation, the symbolic authority of the father as a proxy, or the institutional procedure it invokes as non-material actants that shape and orient the exchange. These discursive forms, though lacking physical presence, are treated as real and consequential in the interaction, demonstrating how 'objects' in this study extend beyond tangible artefacts to include abstract semiotic and institutional formations. This is a figurational relationship, according to Manning (2017, p. 231), where language (the conversation) and non-language (the document) work in tandem to produce meaning and action in a shared semiotic space. The document is not just a static object, but a semiotic act that becomes meaningful in the context of the social ritual of the transaction. The materiality of the document is thus both a literal and figurative actant in the network of the transaction.

This understanding resonates with Appadurai's (2015) view of mediation and materiality. Appadurai asserts that mediation and materiality are inseparable; mediation produces materiality as its effect, and materiality is the site through which the operations of mediation reveal meaning. The power of attorney, in this case, is an embodiment of mediation (i.e., it is a material object that holds significance not in isolation, but through its function in this specific practice). Yet, alongside the physical document, the abstract legal structures it invokes – like authority, representation, and transferability – circulate within the discourse and mediate relations as forcefully as the paper itself. It is through this legal document that the process of selling the land is mediated, both materially and symbolically, between the shop-owners and the person handling the sale. As Appadurai notes, materiality (the document) does not pre-exist the mediation (the delegation of responsibility), and this dynamic interaction between materiality and mediation shapes the way this transaction unfolds. Here, the material semiotic relationship is strongly indexical, where the document and the language exchanged are tied through both pragmatic figuration and iconicity. The material object (the document) and the language exchanged create a semiotic ecology (Manning, 2017) in this context of delegation.

This semiotic ecology is not limited to objects in the narrow physical sense. It encompasses a broader spectrum of actants such as imagined roles (e.g., the father as legal agent), institutional logics (e.g., real estate and bureaucratic norms), and abstract legal categories (e.g., 'ownership' or 'transferability'), all of which mediate social and transactional relations. These include both tangible entities such as documents and conceptual forms like the notion of 'giving power' or the imagined presence of an agent. Structured by conventionalised ties between material artefacts and discursive practices, the document in this context not only mediates the transaction but also acts as a participant in delegation, embodying indexical and iconic relations.

It is here that Pennycook's posthumanist applied linguistics comes into play, emphasising the materiality of the world and the non-human actants involved in language practices. In this interaction, language is not merely a medium for human communication, but a tool that connects humans with the material world and non-human entities (such as the power of attorney). Language becomes a vehicle for mediating material practices, extending beyond human-centred frameworks. The power of attorney, as a tangible material object, enables language practices to produce practical effects, acting as a bridge between human agency and legal materiality. Simultaneously, abstract legal notions – such as 'authority' 'ownership', 'responsibility', and 'representation' – function as immaterial, but agentive, elements that structure the interaction and shape possible outcomes. These are not secondary or derivative; rather, they are constitutive forces within the exchange. This illustrates how indexical and iconic figurations (Harkness, 2015) are at work within this exchange, where the power of attorney becomes a material semiotic form linking human agency to the non-human world, creating a network of actants that shapes the transaction. The pragmatic aspects of language and the materiality of objects in this case highlight a sustained figurational relationship that emerges through both indexical and iconic connections, providing a dynamic understanding of agency and materiality as intertwined in human interaction.

Shifting focus to a new interaction in Extract 4, we encounter another instance where material forces, such as humidity, shape both human actions and the handling of objects. In this case, the customer's question about shelled walnuts prompts the shop-owner to explain how environmental conditions affect their storage practices, which shows the role of material factors in decision-making.

Extract 4

C: A Persian-speaking customer in his mid-50s
SOH: The Shop-owner, the husband

1	C	گردوی باز ندارین.
		Do you have any shelled walnuts?
2	SOH	نه اینجا چون رطوبت وجود داره برای همین ما سعی می کنیم گردوها مون در بسته بمونه و باز نشه چو بو میگیره.
		No, we don't, because of the humidity here. We make sure to keep our walnuts sealed so they don't open and absorb any smell.
3	C	اهان
		got you

In Extract 4, a regular Persian-speaking customer interacts with a shop-owner, enquiring about shelled walnuts. The shop-owner responds by explaining that, due to the high humidity in Sydney, they keep the walnuts sealed to prevent them from absorbing unwanted smells. This explanation points to the influence of material and environmental factors such as humidity and packaging on everyday decisions in the shop. Importantly, these elements do not operate in isolation or merely background the human interaction. Rather, these material and environmental conditions form part of a broader assemblage comprising multiple human and non-human entities: the humidity, the sealed packaging, the walnuts themselves, and even the physical space (the floor and the air) where the interaction takes place. Each of these entities plays a distinctive role in shaping the interaction, but their agency and influence vary depending on their capacities and modes of participation.

Following an actor-network perspective, both humidity and the sealed packaging function as actants that co-produce meaning and material practice. Humidity, as an environmental force, predominantly shapes the conditions under which human and non-human actors operate, exerting a background pressure that constrains and influences decisions and practices without direct intervention in the conversation. Meanwhile, the packaging acts more directly by mediating the relationship between the walnuts, their environment, and the customer, participating actively in the unfolding interaction by preserving the walnuts' quality and symbolising order and cleanliness. Together, they form an assemblage of interdependent entities, as described by Deleuze and Guattari (1987), where human and non-human elements coalesce to produce specific outcomes: the walnuts' quality, the shop-owner's reasoning, and the customer's understanding of the interaction.

The packaging, through its materiality, protects the walnuts from the 'danger' of humidity, a force that destabilises the walnuts' intended order (dry, fresh, and odour-free), thus maintaining the integrity of the assemblage. This dual agency aligns with Mary Douglas' (2002) concept of 'dirt' as 'matter out of place'. In this context, humidity symbolises disorder, which threatens the structured environment of the shop and its goods. The packaging acts as a symbolic and material ritual to restore order, akin to Douglas' argument that systems of purity and pollution reflect larger cultural classifications and practices. By sealing the walnuts, the shop-owner enacts a 'cleansing' ritual to ward off the 'pollution' of unwanted smells and moisture. This highlights how material (humidity) and symbolic practices (cleanliness/order) are interconnected. Just as Douglas argued that dirt reinforces social classifications, here the shop-owner's actions highlight the broader cultural logic of food preservation and environmental adaptation, emphasising the interplay of material forces and symbolic systems.

Crucially, this interaction allows us to distinguish between entities that are merely talked about and those that actively participate in or shape the conversation itself.[1] The walnuts serve as the topic of enquiry (referents that anchor the exchange), but they do not structure the logic of the interaction. In contrast, the roles of humidity and packaging are qualitatively different: they are not only referenced but invoked as causal agents. That is, they are mobilised by the shop-owner to justify his storage practices, and in doing so, they shape both the material action and the conversational trajectory. This contrast illustrates that within an assemblage, not all actants contribute in the same way, nor do they exert the same semiotic or material force.

To sharpen this distinction, we can consider how non-human participants in this assemblage differ in their forms of agency. Some such as the sealed packaging are explicitly named and semiotically loaded, functioning as discursively symbolic participants. The packaging not only preserves the walnuts but also conveys a symbolic order tied to cleanliness, containment, and professionalism. Others (e.g., humidity) operate at the level of environmental conditioning. While not always foregrounded in discourse, humidity sets the material parameters under which other agents must operate, influencing decisions and behaviours through ambient pressure. Still others such as the floor and the air function as latent ambient participants: unnamed, unmarked, yet

---

[1] I am grateful to one of the anonymous reviewers for drawing my attention to the importance of these less visible elements in the assemblage.

materially necessary to the enactment of the interaction. Their agency is non-discursive, shaping the space in which action unfolds. In this way, we can propose a tripartite but overlapping classification of non-human participation (Sayes, 2014): the discursively symbolic (e.g., the sealed packaging), the condition-setting (e.g., humidity), and the latent ambient (e.g., the floor and air). While the packaging is explicitly referenced and imbued with symbolic and moral significance, humidity surfaces only when necessary to explain a choice, for example, its influence otherwise backgrounded. The floor and the air, in contrast, remain unnamed, yet they structure the encounter by enabling movement, proximity, and co-presence. Recognising this range of participation allows us to move beyond reductive accounts of materiality and instead attend to the variable salience, intentionality, and semiotic visibility of actants in situated practice.

While the previous interaction illustrates the intertwined roles of material and symbolic forces in shaping discourse, Extract 5 offers another example where material objects, in this case saffron, actively mediate communication, shaping both linguistic practices and cultural knowledge. In Extract 5, the interaction occurs at the counter, where a Persian shop-owner engages with an Indian couple who have travelled 50 kilometres specifically to this shop to purchase saffron. C1 and C2 are a married couple originally from India, and they regularly shop at this Persian store. In a brief conversation before the recorded interaction, they expressed their appreciation for the shop, not only because its products resonate with their own cultural practices, but also due to the warmth and friendliness of the shop-owners. I had the opportunity to speak with them before and after the recorded interaction, which provided additional context for their engagement with the shop-owner's expertise. This exchange is shaped by both linguistic and material practices, as saffron functions as a mediational tool – not merely a commodity but an active participant in the interaction. Rather than being a passive object, saffron mediates cultural transmission, embedding itself within the discourse as an actant that structures communication and shapes social dynamics. The shop-owner's detailed instructions on preserving and preparing saffron (lines 6–7, 9, 17, 23) illustrate how the substance actively shapes the exchange, influencing both the shop-owner's discourse and the couple's understanding of its value and use. The couple's initial lack of knowledge about grinding saffron (lines 10, 14, 16) highlights how objects themselves generate epistemic shifts, prompting adjustments in human practice. As Latour (1996a, 1996b, 2005) contends, objects act within networks of relations, not as passive entities, or mere *intermediaries* but as *mediators* that actively shape socio-material assemblages.

Extract 5

C1: a male customer
C2: a female customer
SOW: shop-owner ((the wife))
(.) a very short pause
(()): researcher's comment

1	C1	Just because of the saffron we came from really far. Fifty kilometers from here.
2	SOW	oh where are you living?
3	C1	Rockdale ((a suburb in Sydney))
4	SOW	oh (.) far away (.) Is that credit?
5	C1	Yes, credit
6	SOW	You can keep in the freezer or fridge. You have to put it in the freezer or fridge.
7	C2	Oh OK
8	SOW	yeah. That way it keeps the colour and smell for a long time. CW and C are now talking to each other in Panjabi.
9	SOW	Just ground ((she means grind it)) it very finely, you know how to use it?
10	C1	We only use it with milk
11	SOW	because that way
12	C1	and then we of course fill it with milk
13	SOW	If you ground ((grind)) it
14	C1	It's better or?
15	SOW	Much better
16	C1	Oh I didn't know that
17	SOW	because that way you are wasting, it's very expensive. You have to ground ((grind)) it very finely like that ((showing a ground saffron from the shelf)) and put it in the little jar and keep it in the fridge or freezer.
18	C1	oh that's good.
19	SOW	yeah that way you wasted
20	C1	We just finished one only when she was pregnant.
21	SOW	no no. Just ground ((grind)) it you have a little grinder?
22	C1	yeah
23	SOW	just ground ((grind)) it and put it in the jar in the fridge
24	C1	Thank you, see you later.
25	SOW	Thanks

The interaction highlights how saffron's agency is not only expressed through its material properties but also through the discourse that surrounds its preparation and preservation. The shop-owner's repeated emphasis on grinding saffron (lines 9, 13, 17, 21, 23) illustrates how linguistic and material practices jointly co-constitute meaning, enacting what Sayes (2014) and ANT scholars describe as objects mediating action, rather than merely enabling it. The imperative nature of the shop-owner's directives (e.g., 'You have to put it in the freezer or fridge', line 6; 'Just ground it very finely', line 9) exemplifies how linguistic formulations do not merely describe material actions but actively structure them. These directives, in turn, align with saffron's agency in the interaction, as its preservation and use necessitate precise material and linguistic practices.

Following Sayes' (2014) typology, saffron functions as (1) a condition of sociality, providing a platform for interaction where advice is exchanged, traditions are recalled, and gestures of care are enacted such as discussions about authenticity, proper use, or sourcing; (2) a mediator of action, shaping everyday culinary routines by introducing new affordances and constraints, from careful storage in the fridge to the symbolic weight it adds to a dish; and (3) a participant in a moral-political assemblage, entangled in discourses of gendered care, domestic responsibility, and cultural value, where its presence signals attentiveness, generosity, or propriety in household management. In this network, the fridge acts as an important actant, not merely storing saffron but actively maintaining its potency and reinforcing the shop-owner's epistemic authority.

This interplay underscores how material objects mediate discourse, a dynamic captured in scholarship on language materiality (Cavanaugh & Shankar, 2014; Shankar & Cavanaugh, 2017), which emphasises that linguistic forms are deeply embedded within material realities. The shop-owner's use of gestures to demonstrate the grinding process (line 17) further solidifies this relationship, reinforcing how language operates through embodied and object-oriented practices rather than merely serving as a vehicle for abstract knowledge. The epistemological configuration that emerges here is distributed: knowledge is not housed in the shop-owner alone but co-produced through her interactions with saffron, the fridge, the grinder, and the couple's prior practices. This reflects ANT's commitment to distributed agency and Sayes' claim that attributing agency to nonhumans involves tracing their entanglement in social relations.

Saffron's agency in this interaction is not only realised through its material properties and linguistic framing but also through the shifting configurations of human and nonhuman elements that shape everyday transactions. The Indian couple, the shop-owner, and the saffron itself form a dynamic assemblage in which each element influences the others. The couple's prior use of saffron in milk (line 10) signifies an existing culinary practice, yet the shop-owner's directives (lines 9, 13, 17, 21) reconfigure this assemblage by positioning grinding as essential to saffron's potency. Alongside grinding, the directive to store saffron in the fridge (line 6) adds another layer to this assemblage, illustrating how human and nonhuman actants collaborate in the construction of culinary knowledge. This transformation is not unilateral but emerges from the interplay of discourse and materiality, aligning with Deleuze and Guattari's (1987) notion of assemblages as fluid networks of relations. The shop-owner's knowledge, which draws from Persian culinary traditions, does not merely inform but actively restructures the couple's engagement with saffron, demonstrating how objects, far from passive, shape human practices (Miller, 2005). Crucially, this transformation is dialogic (Bakhtin, 1982; Blommaert, 2010) rather than one-directional. The couple's participation, their questions (lines 14, 16) and responses ('Oh, I didn't know that', line 16; 'That's good', line 18), demonstrates an active negotiation of meaning rather than passive reception. The shop-owner's repeated insistence on grinding (lines 9, 13, 21) reflects a culturally embedded epistemology, in which material preparation is integral to culinary authenticity. Similarly, the instruction to refrigerate saffron situates it within a broader framework of preservation practices, where technological infrastructures (e.g., refrigeration) become entangled with traditional knowledge, reinforcing the mutual dependence of discourse and materiality.

From this perspective, saffron operates as a mediant, co-constructed through its embeddedness in cultural and material contexts (Appadurai, 2015). This analysis underscores how saffron, as an actant, actively structures discourse and practice, reinforcing the interdependence of language, materiality, and assemblages. Rather than simply transmitting cultural knowledge, the interaction reveals how such knowledge is dynamically reconstituted through engagements with material objects (Latour, 1996a, 1996b). In this case, saffron is not merely a commodity; it is an agent that mediates, influences and restructures culinary practice and cultural exchange. This perspective aligns with the broader literature on language materiality (Cavanaugh & Shankar, 2014; Shankar & Cavanaugh, 2017) and assemblage theory (Deleuze & Guattari, 1987; Miller, 2005), further illustrating how material objects serve as mediants in the ongoing negotiation of cultural practices. This shift exemplifies how mediants evolve within assemblages, influenced by the interplay of human agency and material affordances. Such a transformation exemplifies the evolving role of mediants within assemblages, shaped by the interplay of human agency and material affordances. This discussion of saffron's agency within assemblages and its role as a mediant in cultural and material exchanges sets the stage for a broader examination of discourse and materiality in everyday interactions.

The next section expands this analysis by exploring how objects mediate transactional encounters and contribute to the negotiation of social and cultural meanings in commercial settings.

5 Entangling Discourse, Materiality, and Identity in Diasporic Service Encounters

Interactions in commercial spaces, such as service encounters, offer a rich site for analysing how language and materiality intersect. These exchanges are not merely transactional; rather, they are moments where cultural meanings are negotiated, contested, and reaffirmed. Through an analysis of Extracts 6–12, I examine how objects such as dates function as mediators in social interactions, revealing their capacity to structure discourse, shape participant dynamics, and contribute to the construction of cultural and material meanings.

Extract 6

Language guide: regular font = **English**; italics = **Persian**; bold = **researcher's ethnographic notes**
SOH: shop-owner (the husband)
FC: female customer (Anglo-Australian)
SOW (shop-owner's wife)
MC (male customer: Persian-speaking customer)

1	SOH	((**FC putting the items on the counter**)) thank you
2	FC	are these ones ((**pointing to the dates at the counter**)) to taste
3	SOH	yeah ((**his voice is fading as if he was reluctant to answer**))
4	FC	yeah I'll have one they're different ((**SO is busy bagging**))
5	SOH	that's a fresh date ((**maintaining eye contact while handing the receipt and the change to FC**))
6	FC	((**while eating**)) hm ((**nodding**))
		10 seconds later ((**FC is grabbing the items along with the receipt and the change**))
7	FC	thank you
8	SOW	thank you ((**sitting behind the counter, busy watching a program on her laptop**))
		((**a new customer brings an item to the counter and SO is busy serving him**))

Extract 6 presents an interaction between two customers (a Persian-speaking male and a female Anglo-Australian), both in their early thirties, and the shop-owner, which is characteristic of the 'service encounter' genre. The exchange revolves around business-oriented talk with a clear focus on achieving transactional goals, exemplifying what Bailey (2000) describes as a 'socially minimal service encounter' (lines 1–8). However, such exchanges also serve as microcosms of larger socio-cultural dynamics, where objects, language, and participants reflect and reproduce cultural differences and intersections. Central to this interaction is the date, which at first glance might seem like a straightforward consumable item. Yet, when examined through the frameworks of actant theory (Latour, 2005), objectification (Miller, 2005), and the social life of things (Appadurai, 1986, 2015), the date reveals itself as a dynamic participant in the encounter, mediating cultural and social exchanges while shaping the interaction's flow and meaning.

In this encounter, the date functions as a mediational means (Scollon, 2001), mediating the interaction between the shop-owner and the female customer. FC's enquiry in line 2, 'are these ones to taste?' initiates an engagement with the date as an object of sensory curiosity and consumption (see Figure 3). By tasting the date (line 6), FC engages with it as a tangible, embodied experience. This aligns with Appadurai's (1986) concept of how objects mediate cultural and economic flows. This sensory engagement is not merely an individual act but a linguistic and material negotiation, where the customer's question frames the date as an uncertain object whose meaning needs to be discursively and materially constructed. This aligns with Shankar and Cavanaugh's (2012) view of the material dimensions of language, in which meaning emerges through interactional and semiotic processes that incorporate both discourse and the physical presence of objects. This sensory engagement is significant, as it blurs the boundaries between object and subject, bringing the embodied experience of taste into a shared social moment. The act of tasting itself

Figure 3 The dates on the counter

becomes a culturally charged ritual (Mondada, 2018), particularly for FC, who might associate it with exploratory consumption, an act that situates her as both a participant in and an outsider to the cultural practice. For the Anglo-Australian FC, the date is likely perceived as an exotic product, one that symbolises a connection to a cultural realm outside her immediate experience. This perception of the date as 'exotic' may shape FC's approach to the interaction, framing the act of consumption not only as an exploration of taste but also as a deeper engagement with cultural difference. This creates a moment of tasting that introduces a layer of cultural negotiation, positioning the date as a mediator between two worlds.

Yet, the date is not merely a static commodity here. From the perspective of actor-network theory (Latour, 2005), the date emerges as an actant within this interaction, actively influencing the dynamics of the exchange. By shaping SOH's response, both his reluctant tone (line 3) and his emphasis on freshness (line 5), the date asserts itself as an influential presence in the interaction. The shop-owner's hesitation in line 3 can be interpreted as a moment of ambivalence, perhaps reflecting concerns about the customer's genuine interest in the date or scepticism about the potential wastage of a sample. This hesitation might also indicate a broader anxiety about Western perceptions of ethnic products, raising questions about authenticity and the value of 'exotic' goods in a multicultural marketplace. His emphasis on freshness is not simply a descriptor but an invocation of cultural and economic value, reinforcing the ways in which linguistic and material signs co-construct meaning in service encounters. The notion of 'freshness' itself resonates with discourses of capital and labour, where food marketing strategies and commodity fetishism (Harvey, 1990) imbue certain food items with an aura of authenticity and value, which loosely aligns them with notions of quality and cultural heritage (Izadi, 2020; Johnston & Baumann, 2014; Pietikäinen et al., 2016). The shop-owner's somewhat reluctant response (line 3) and the subsequent emphasis on the date's freshness (line 5) reflect the date's capacity to shape not only the transactional flow but also the relational dynamics between the participants. The date mediates the shop-owner's role as an expert in cultural knowledge and the customer's position as a curious customer, subtly highlighting the asymmetry of their cultural positioning. This asymmetry is often present in cross-cultural service encounters, where ethnic products are subject to external perceptions of authenticity and value (Miller, 2005).

In this case, FC's positioning as an outsider reinforces power dynamics, as her engagement with the date is framed as a cultural exploration or exotic experience, which can reinforce the notion of 'ethnic' products as distinct from mainstream consumption. This perception of 'exoticism' underscores the tensions between the familiar and the foreign in consumer experiences, as FC's consumption is framed as an exploration of cultural difference rather than as a routine act of purchasing. This asymmetry, however, is mitigated by the shared act of exchange, where the date facilitates not just communication but a temporary bridging of cultural identities. In doing so, the date becomes a liminal object, rooted in Iranian culture yet accessible through a universal sensory mode (taste) that transcends cultural barriers. Through this layered analysis, the date is revealed as a complex and multifaceted participant in the interaction, mediating sensory, cultural, and ritual dimensions. It exemplifies the entanglement of material objects with human practices, reminding us that even routine service encounters are rich with socio-cultural meaning, shaped by the interplay of objects, actors, and shared contexts. Moreover, the shop space itself contributes to the semiotic cues within the interaction. The placement of the dates near the counter invites engagement (see Figure 3), positioning the dates not only as a commodity for sale but also as a culturally significant item. This positioning reinforces the role of dates as a mediational means, encouraging customers to enquire and engage with them in ways that highlight their cultural significance.

The dates are imbued with deeper layers of meaning, functioning not only as sensory items for tasting and potential purchase but also as symbols with profound significance in Iranian cultural and religious practices. In this instance, the dates are placed on the counter to honour the passing of a Persian customer's father, which reflects the tradition of distributing dates as part of condolence rituals on Thursday nights. This practice illustrates the symbolic role of dates in Persian mourning customs and highlights the performative nature of material culture, where the act of giving or consuming dates reinforces communal bonds and enacts shared cultural values. As customers engage with the dates, they also engage with the cultural and discursive practices surrounding them, extending the material performativity into linguistic space. In doing so, the dates move beyond their practical function, becoming active participants in the ongoing construction of meaning and identity. At the same time, the dates also serve a dual role: they are objects of curiosity for Anglo-Australian customers and ritualistic symbols of remembrance for Persian customers. This dual function emphasises Miller's (2005) concept of objectification, where material objects like dates actively shape and reflect social and cultural values, identities, and relationships. By mediating sensory, cultural, and ritual dimensions, the dates transcend their practical role, embodying the intersection of local and global flows of meaning, value, and identity. Through their use in ritual and exchange, the dates demonstrate how even mundane objects can transcend their practical purpose, actively participating in the construction of meaning and reflecting the dynamic power of material culture.

Extract 7 emphasises the intersection of cultural practices and social roles, particularly in a diasporic context. The date transforms from being a consumable item for business purposes (as seen in Extract 6) to a culturally charged symbol of mourning. The shop-owner's role shifts here; he is not only a seller of goods but also a custodian of ritual space. The dates on the counter are no longer simply items for sale but become carriers of memory and commemoration, facilitating an exchange that is beyond commerce. This act of placing ritualistic objects in commercial space illustrates how diasporic settings often blur the boundaries between the sacred and the secular, which creates spaces for both economic activity and cultural practice to coexist. This act of placing dates on the counter in honour of the deceased customer's father (see Izadi, 2020) signifies a communal and ritualistic act of solidarity, with the object itself becoming a tool for collective memory and the ritualistic bonding of community. Here, Ahmed's (2014) concept of 'sticky objects' is particularly illuminating: the date, as a material object, becomes affectively charged through its association with mourning, memory, and cultural attachment. It 'sticks' not only to the event of death but to broader diasporic experiences of loss, belonging, and ritual practice.

The customer's question, 'Are you giving dates to charity?' (line 9), is framed humorously and reflects his awareness of the ritual significance of dates. However, his suggestion that the dates might be given to charity 'for the new president' (line 9) introduces a playful misunderstanding. The Persian-speaking customer, familiar with charitable practices involving dates, humorously juxtaposes the ritual act of giving dates with a contemporary political context. His tone shifts from humour to a more respectful one (lines 11–13) upon learning the true purpose of the dates, revealing a deeper understanding of their cultural meaning. In this exchange, the dates serve as a hybrid object, one that simultaneously embodies charity and a ritual object for mourning. Their emotional and symbolic resonance reinforces their 'stickiness' as Ahmed describes, circulating in the shop space not just as goods but as affectively loaded artefacts shaped by both individual memory and shared cultural meanings. This highlights how cultural practices surrounding objects can be both humorous and serious, depending on the context in which they are interpreted. This interplay between humour and solemnity underscores the fluid nature of cultural symbols, where meanings are context-dependent and negotiated through interaction. The customer's comment highlights how objects like dates can be subject to different interpretations based on cultural references, blending political, charitable, and ritualistic meanings.

Extract 7

Language guide: regular font = **English**; italics = **Persian**; bold = **researcher's ethnographic notes**
SOH: shop-owner (the husband)
MC (male customer: Persian-speaking customer)

9	MC	*khorma(.)kheyrati midin↑(.)bara chiye↑=bara raees jomhoriye↑*
		are you giving dates to charity what are they for for the new president **((smiling))**
10	SOH	*=na=ye aghayee pedaresh foot karde(.) sa[le*
		no they're for someone whose father passed away and he bought them in commemoration of his
11	MC	*aha ee]*
		oh I see **((MC suddenly changed his voice as if he was embarrassed))**
12	SOH	*pedaresh bood (.)*
		it was his father
13	MC	*ee khoda rahmatesh kone*
		Oh may he rest in peace
		((SO is bagging the bought items))
14	SOH	*(4.0) behesh goftam=goftam inja bezari baziya fekr mikonan male sampele(.)*
		I told him that if he bought a box of dates and put it at the counter people would think it's a sample
15	MC	*Are*
		yes you're right
16	SOH	*khorma gozashtim=baziya(.)mikhorano(.)migan agha in kara chiye*
		so I've put the dates here some are eating and saying 'what is it'
		=baziya ham mikhoran fateh ham mikhonan
		and some are eating and are praying for him **((for the guidance, lordship and mercy of God))**
17	MC	*=ahan*
		I see
18	SOH	*=Goft man niyatam moheme*
		he **((the customer whose father passed away))** said he wanted to do it for his father
		to bezar=goftam bashe
		and asked me to put the dates at the counter and I said sure
19	MC	*bashe hhh*
		yeah sure **((laughing))**
20	SOH	*man poolesho migiram mizaram=kari nadaram↓hhh*
		as long as he pays for the dates, I'll leave them there at the counter I don't care **(smiling)**

The interaction also reveals the material and social pragmatics of the ritual. The shop-owner's explanation (lines 14–16) of how the dates are placed out for others to sample and how some customers eat them while others say prayers further illustrates how the dates perform multiple functions, facilitating social interaction, fostering ritual observance, and acting as mediators of social relationships. The dates, then, are not merely passive items for consumption; they are active participants in the social ritual of mourning, blending the practical (the transaction) with the symbolic (the act of remembrance and prayer). This dual functionality highlights how material objects mediate between the personal and collective, creating opportunities for individual acts of remembrance while reinforcing shared cultural practices. In addition, the shop-owner's comment that 'as long as he pays for the dates, I'll leave them there at the counter' (line 20) adds a layer of pragmatism to the ritual. It shows the negotiation of ritual and commercial interests within the everyday practices of the shop. Despite the deeply symbolic significance of the dates, the shop-owner's position suggests a pragmatic view of ritual. He is willing to accommodate the cultural practice of the customer but remains rooted in the business transaction. This tension between economic pragmatism and cultural accommodation reveals the complexities of navigating diasporic identities, where the preservation of cultural practices must often coexist with the realities of commercial life. This dynamic highlights the tension between cultural respect and market realities, where objects, such as dates, become vessels for both cultural practice and commercial exchange. Moreover, the dates in this context also demonstrate cultural hybridity. The fusion of Persian mourning practices with Australian commercial exchange creates a space where cross-cultural meanings are negotiated, contested, and reinterpreted. The shop itself, as a site of transaction, becomes a site of cultural convergence, where the global and local intersect (Blommaert, 2010). The ritual use of dates as part of Persian mourning practices within the context of an Australian corner shop exemplifies how objects can embody multidimensional roles, simultaneously fulfilling cultural, ritualistic, and commercial functions.

The previous discussion on the material and social pragmatics of dates within the mourning ritual highlights how objects can serve multiple, interrelated functions. In Extract 8, we shift focus from the material culture of ritual to the discursive practices that shape diasporic identities and political memories. The customer's narrative about the Iranian Revolution of 1979 illustrates how historical events continue to resonate in the present through conversation, memory, and material artefacts.

In Extract 8, a Persian-speaking customer (in his mid-fifties), a long-time resident of Sydney (twenty-five years at the time of recording) and a taxi driver, wearing his uniform, steers the conversation toward the Iranian Revolution of 1979, particularly focusing on Ayatollah Khomeini's return from exile in Paris. The customer recalls Ayatollah Khomeini's arrival in Tehran and his first speech at Beheshte Zahra, a significant cemetery in Tehran where he addressed his supporters. This moment in history is not just a political event but a site of discursive struggle, where promises, expectations, and ideological shifts were set in motion, which has shaped the trajectories of Iranian society. The customer's account is not merely an anecdote but an instance of historical intertextuality, where past political discourse resurfaces in the present, mediated through conversation, memory, and material artefacts.

Extract 8

مشتری: همون روز اول آوردنش تهرون، الان او نواری که تو بهشت زهرا صحبت کرده از هر کی بگیرنش اعدامش می کنن. از هر کی بگیرن . . . برای اینکه می گفت پول نفت نباید بدین تکس نباید بدیم، پول برق نباید بدیم. می گفتن مملکت با چی بچرخه، می گفتن اقتصاد، می گفت اقتصاد مال خره، سواد این آقا این بود دیگه.

Following is the translation of the previous Persian text.
Customer: On the very first day (upon his return from exile in Paris), they (Ayatollah Khomeini's supporters) brought him to Tehran. Now, that tape of him speaking at Behesht Zahra (a famous cemetery in Tehran where Ayatollah Khomeini went directly upon his return and addressed his supporters) if they catch anyone with it, they'll execute them. If they even find the tape on someone . . . because he was saying we shouldn't pay for oil, we shouldn't pay taxes, we shouldn't pay for electricity. They would ask, 'Then how will the country function?' They would talk about the economy, and he would say, 'The economy is for donkeys'. That was his level of knowledge.

Ayatollah Khomeini's speech contained radical economic promises, asserting that Iranians would no longer have to pay for essential services such as gas, electricity, and water. The speech was recorded and widely disseminated on cassette tapes, turning these tapes into potent political artefacts. However, as political power consolidated, the very act of possessing such a tape became criminalised. This transformation exemplifies Latour's (2005) concept of the actant, in which the cassette is not a neutral object but an active participant in shaping historical and political realities. The cassette, in this context, is not merely a passive carrier of information but an object with agency, its presence implicates individuals in networks of resistance, state surveillance, and potential persecution. It shifts from a medium of revolutionary fervour to a mediator of state control, marking those who own it as threats to the regime.

From the perspective of Scollon's (2001) mediational means, the cassette operates within multiple semiotic cycles: first, as a revolutionary tool that propagates ideology; later, as a subversive artefact that signals dissent. The materiality of the cassette itself (small, portable, and replicable) allows it to slip through state controls, making it a tool of covert circulation. Yet, its very portability becomes its liability: its discovery can lead to imprisonment, and as the customer claims, even execution. Unlike the credit card in Extract 2, which exposes private actions within the commercial sphere, the cassette intervenes in the political domain, materialising both resistance and repression. To fully appreciate the entanglement of materiality, discourse, and language in this instance, we must consider how objects function as both semiotic and political agents. As Miller (2005) argues, materiality is not simply about physical substances but also about the socio-cultural forces embedded in them. The cassette, as an artefact, carries layers of meaning that extend beyond its physicality; it serves as a discursive object, deeply interwoven with a network of political and social contestation. Drawing on Bourdieu's (1977b) concept of practice, the cassette shapes and is shaped by social structures. It functions as both a medium of resistance and a tool of oppression, depending on the socio-political context in which it circulates.

In light of this, the materiality of language itself must be considered in this interaction. Language does not function in isolation but is materially instantiated in physical forms whether as cassette tapes, written texts, or embodied speech (Shankar & Cavanaugh, 2017). The cassette, in this case, is not just a medium for words; it actively materialises discourse, making it tangible and, therefore, vulnerable to state intervention. As Järlehed et al. (2023) argue, language materiality foregrounds how discourse operates through physical media, shaping political economies and social hierarchies. In this way, the cassette exemplifies how linguistic materiality operates within broader structures of power, where access to and control over discourse are tightly regulated. The customer's narrative, then, is more than a historical recollection. It is an engagement with the material-discursive entanglements that continue to shape perceptions of history and governance. His critique of Ayatollah Khomeini's economic promises is not simply a matter of ideological disagreement but a reflection on how discourse materialises through objects and circulates within networks of power. This perspective aligns with Barad's (2003) posthumanist performativity, which challenges the separation of language and materiality, instead emphasising their co-constitutive nature. In this interaction, discourse is not merely spoken; it is embedded in material artefacts, shaping and being shaped by the socio-political landscape in which it unfolds. Thus, the cassette is more than just an archival object; rather, it is an ideological actant, entangling individuals in networks of power, surveillance, and historical memory. Its presence in this interaction underscores the ongoing negotiation of political identity, as the customer engages in a retrospective critique of a promise unfulfilled. By integrating theories of materiality, discourse, and language, we see how objects are not passive carriers of meaning but active participants in shaping historical and political realities.

Given the intertwined relationship between material objects and social practices, as illustrated by the cassette, Extract 9 further demonstrates how material culture (specifically the act of tea preparation) becomes a medium for expressing cultural identity and social memory. The customer's enquiry about loose-leaf tea, initially appearing as a simple transactional question, serves as a subtle act of indexing Persian tea culture. By referencing loose-leaf tea, the customer invokes a shared cultural script that contrasts with the dominant tea-drinking practices in Australia, where tea bags are more common. This seemingly ordinary question thus establishes an implicit cultural boundary. It reinforces the distinctiveness of Persian tea traditions in contrast to dominant Australian tea-drinking practices.

Extract 9

C: A Persian-speaking customer in her late 40s
SOW: shop-owner (the wife)

1	C	شما چای دمی دارین؟
		Do you have loose leaf tea?
2	SOW	اره
		Yes
3	C	اره اینا چقدر حال میداد اونموقعها
		Yes, those good old days.
4	SOW	عطر داشت
		It had an authentic aroma.
5		عطر داشت الان همش انگار خاکه اینجوری نیس دم بکشه. قبلا اول آب رو تو سماور میذاشتن تا جوش بیاد بد چای رو میذاشتن تو قوری بالای سماور دم بیکشه بدش دور هم میشستن و چایی میخوردن و گپ میزدن
		It had a scent; now it feels like dust, it doesn't brew the same way. Before ((C means back in Iran)), they would first put the water in the samovar to boil, then they would put the tea in the teapot on top of the samovar to brew. And then they would sit together, drink tea, and chat.
6	SWO	((نامفهوم))
		((Inaudible))
7	C	چون سریع هستیم باید دم بکشه رنگ بیگیره. من مهمون هم دارم میزارم تو چیزا زیرشم روشن میکنم رنگ بگیر سریع رنگ بدم به مهمونا. همون قسمت بخش چای هست. یه نگاه میکنم البته باید بزارم رو گاز دیگه. سیستم اینجوری مثل ایران که نیست

		Because we're in a hurry, the tea must brew so it gets the right colour. When I have guests, I'll place the tea in the teapot under the heater, turn it on to brew and get the colour, and quickly check on the guests to serve them. The tea section is over there ((The customer is leaving the counter to the place where the teapots are located)). I'll take a quick look, but I have to put it on the stove. Right? The setup here isn't like it is in Iran.
8	SWO	یا بزارین تو در این کتریها
		Or you can put the tea on the lid of these kettles here
9	C	اهان از در دوقلوها اره یعنی پیرکس باشه
		Ah, you can place the teapot on the lid of these kettles here to brew the tea., yes, meaning it should be Pyrex.
10	SWO	اره
		Yes

It is within this context that the customer recalls 'those good old days' (line 3), a phrase that does more than simply reference the past. Rather than a neutral recollection, this moment frames the past as an idealised temporality, positioning it in contrast to the present. The shop-owner immediately aligns with this comment, reinforcing it through sensory memory: 'It had an authentic aroma' (line 4). This alignment not only strengthens the nostalgic framing of the past but also establishes a discursive act of authentication (Karrebæk & Maegaard, 2024). By emphasising the sensory qualities of Persian tea, the shop-owner implicitly differentiates traditional tea from contemporary alternatives, invoking authenticity through embodied experience. This act of authentication is further developed through the discussion of tea preparation. The mention of the samovar, an iconic object in Persian tea culture (see further), functions as more than a reference to a brewing method; it conjures a material and social world where tea-drinking extends beyond individual consumption. The recollection of a collective tea-drinking ritual, 'They would sit together, drink tea, and chat' (line 5), demonstrates how the samovar (Figure 4) serves as a mediational means that structures social interaction. In the context of Persian tea-drinking rituals, tea is not merely a beverage, but a *practice* embedded in hospitality and extended conversation. The shift from the samovar to modern kettles signals more than a technological change; it also transforms the tempo of social life. While the samovar structured communal engagement, the modern kettle suggests a different temporality and mode of social organisation, raising questions about how material culture mediates shifting social relations.

Historical context further reinforces the material-discursive dimension of this analysis. The samovar, central to the discussion, was originally a Russian invention from the eighteenth century, and as the modern Iranian historian Firaydun Adamiyat (1354/1975) has argued (an assertion frequently cited in

Figure 4 An earlier version of the samovar

Iranian historiography), tea began to be imported into Iran with the introduction of samovars during the tenure of the Qajar chief minister Amir Kabir in the late 1840s (see also Matthee, 1996). It performs three functions at once: boiling water, dispensing hot water through a spout, and keeping the tea warm by placing the teapot on top. Over time, the samovar became deeply embedded in Persian tea culture, where it is now seen as an emblem of hospitality and tradition. Tea itself, called *chai* in Iran, arrived via the Silk Road, tracing a linguistic and cultural path from China, where it was originally known as *cha (Adamiyat, 1354/1975)*. This etymological and historical journey reflects the interconnectedness of material culture, language, and trade.

Today, Iranians drink chai throughout the day, and tea is deeply embedded in Persian social life, indexing moments of relaxation, rest, and hospitality. The Persian tea ceremony, in particular, remains an integral part of Iranian identity. This cultural embeddedness, however, becomes a site of tension in migratory contexts, where traditional material practices may no longer be easily sustained. This shift exemplifies what Tannock (1995) terms continuity and discontinuity in nostalgic discourse. While the past is valorised, its absence in the present is foregrounded, which emphasises a sense of cultural dislocation. The customer's comment 'The setup here isn't like it is in Iran' in line 7 marks a moment of explicit contrast between cultural worlds, making visible the ways in which migration disrupts habitual, taken-for-granted practices (Bourdieu, 1977b). The customer's attempt to adapt to new conditions by using a heater to quickly brew tea for guests illustrates how traditional practices are transformed in response to material constraints. Drawing from Bourdieu's (1977b) concept of habitus, the customer and the shop-owner's discussion illustrates how deeply ingrained practices of tea-drinking are shaped by cultural dispositions. These dispositions influence their perceptions of authenticity, where the act of tea preparation and consumption becomes a marker of Persian identity that is reconfigured in the context of migration.

Yet, nostalgia here is not a simple longing for the past, but rather it is actively mobilised to authenticate contemporary practices. Both the customer and the shop-owner position themselves as epistemic authorities on 'real' Persian tea, enacting what Bucholtz and Hall (Bucholtz & Hall, 2005) describe as identity positioning through expertise. The shop-owner, as a vendor of Persian goods, claims a form of institutionalised authenticity, while the customer, by invoking the past, claims experiential authenticity. The interplay between these forms of authority reflects Manning's (2012) notion of discursive chains of authentication, where products, people, and places come together as an assemblage in the semiotic construction of authenticity. The shop itself thus emerges as more than a commercial space; it is a site of cultural reproduction (Bourdieu, 1977a) where Persian identity is (re)negotiated and (re)enacted (Garfinkel, 1967).

The discussion of alternative tea-making methods, particularly the mention of Pyrex kettles (line 9), complicates the binary opposition between tradition and modernity. Rather than being wholly displaced, Persian tea practices are adapted to new material conditions, reflecting a form of 'adaptive' authenticity. The shop-owner's suggestion (line 8) to place the teapot on the lid of a kettle and the customer's confirmation (line 9) reveal a pragmatic response to material constraints, signalling an ongoing negotiation between past and present tea-drinking practices. This moment of negotiation explains the dynamic nature of authenticity itself not a static essence but a semiotic process continually shaped by social and material contingencies (Pietikäinen & Hegel, 2021).

Both the customer and the shop-owner evoke nostalgia as a discursive strategy. The customer recalls the scent of Persian tea and the communal experience of tea-drinking, aligning her memories with a broader cultural script that associates Persian tea with warmth, tradition, and shared experience. The shop-owner, in turn, reinforces this nostalgia by positioning the shop as a space where such traditions can be relived. The links between past, present, and imagined future moments are central to the rhetorical practices of nostalgia (Doane & Hodges, 1987), where both continuity and discontinuity shape the nostalgic experience (Tannock, 1995). The shop provides a universe of interpretation in which Persian identity emerges through a semiotic assemblage (Pietikäinen & Hegel, 2021). Objects such as the samovar, the Pyrex kettle, and the Persian tea itself function as mediational means that co-construct Persian culture as an available and meaningful resource. Customers do not merely purchase items; rather, they engage in a process of meaning-making in which Persian identity is both reaffirmed and transformed through discourse.

The discussion on Persian tea-drinking practices demonstrates key theoretical concerns regarding materiality, agency, and mediation. The samovar, porcelain teapots, and even the tea itself are not passive objects; rather, they actively mediate social interactions and discursive constructions of Persian identity. The shop-owner, in asserting the authenticity of Persian tea, is not simply selling a product but is participating in a broader semiotic economy where material objects serve as anchors for cultural belonging and nostalgia. Appadurai's (1996) concept of 'scapes' (referring to the fluid and disjunctive global flows of people, ideas, and objects) can further illuminate how nostalgia functions in the diaspora. Here, nostalgia is not just a longing for the past but also a means to negotiate one's position within shifting material and social conditions. The customer's attempt to recreate the sensory experiences of Persian tea culture highlights the negotiation of cultural continuity within the disjunctures of migration. By integrating historical, cultural, and theoretical perspectives, this analysis highlights how Persian tea culture is not just about drinking tea but about engaging with a deeply layered semiotic and material world where past and present are continually negotiated.

Shifting the focus to another key area of material culture, the conversation in Extract 10 reveals how food practices, specifically, the sourcing and consumption of meat, serve as a site of cultural negotiation within the diaspora. Here, two Persian-speaking female customers engage in a discussion that not only reflects individual preferences but also brings to the fore broader processes of identity construction, taste, and adaptation to new material conditions in a diasporic setting.

Extract 10

1	C1	شما گوشتتونو از کجا میگیرن؟
		Where do you get your meat from?
2	C2	گوشتو؟
		The meat?
3	C1	حلال می گیرین؟
		Do you get halal?
4	C2	بعضی وقتا حلال می گیریم و بعضی وقتها هم حروم می گیریم. گوشت حلال و حروم و قاطی میکونیم ها، ها، ها
		Sometimes we get halal, and sometimes we get non-halal. We mix halal and non-halal meat. Ha, ha, ha
5	SOW	گوشت حلال و حروم
		Halal and non-halal meat ((her voice carries a critical tone, almost questioning, 'What's the difference between the two'?))

6	C1	آره ببین مزه ی گوشت اینجا با مال ایران فرق می کنه. ما به نسبت تازه اومدیم زمان می بره تا به گوشت اینجا عادت کنیم.
		Yeah, see, The taste of the meat here is different from the taste of the meat in Iran. We've only just arrived, so it takes time to get used to the meat here.
7	SOW	آخه چه گوشتی می گیرین،
		Well, what kind of meat do you get?
8	C1	گوشت گوسفند می گیریم
		We buy lamb
9	SOW	شما برین وولورث گوشت گوسفند بگیرین ادم حظ میکنه میخوره.
		You should go to Woolworths and get lamb; it's really good, you'll enjoy it.
10	C1	ما الان رفتیم بلک تون گوشت گرفتیم.
		We've just gone to Blacktown and got meat.
11	SOW	خوب بلک تون که حلاله.
		Well, Blacktown's meat is halal
12	C1	آره حلاله. ماهیچه اش و، مهناز جون اینا خونه ی ما بودن چند شب پیش، انقدر خوششون آمده بود، که می گفتن واقعاً لذیذه.
13	C2	از کجا؟
		From where?
14	C1	تو بلک تون.
		From Blacktown

The exchange in Extract 10 foregrounds the indexicality of place (Johnstone, 2004) in shaping food choices, particularly in relation to halal authentication and cultural belonging. The reference to Blacktown, a suburb with a significant Arabic-speaking population (4.1 per cent according to the Australian Bureau of Statistics, 2021), immediately situates the conversation within a diasporic foodscape where food consumption is intricately tied to trust, familiarity, and social knowledge (Adekunle & Filson, 2020). Customer 1's enquiry in line 3, 'Do you get halal?' is not simply about dietary restrictions but about the perceived legitimacy of halal meat in a particular market space. The shop-owner's response in line 11, 'Well, Blacktown's meat is halal', rather than assuming the role of an arbiter of authenticity, functions as a pragmatic statement that invokes an assumed collective understanding of Blacktown as a hub for halal consumption. While this response may carry an undertone of critique, suggesting that halal is widely available and not necessarily restricted to Blacktown, it simultaneously reinforces the discursive association between place and authenticity. This spatial distinction between mainstream supermarkets and ethnically specific butchers reflects diasporic consumers' strategic engagement with multiple food economies (Cavanaugh, 2007). In line with Appadurai's (1996) notion of 'scapes', this moment highlights how foodscapes become arenas of cultural continuity and transformation, where shopping choices signal not just dietary preferences but also social class (Maguire, 2016), cultural adaptation, and trust in authenticity.

This moment of authentication is particularly significant in diasporic contexts, where halal consumption operates within overlapping registers of religious practice, cultural continuity, and everyday material conditions. The reference to Blacktown is not just a matter of location but an invocation of a social geography that structures food practices through semiotic and economic distinctions. The spatial dimension of this negotiation is particularly significant, as the conversation contrasts different retail spaces, each with distinct socio-material implications. The shop-owner's suggestion in line 9, 'You should go to Woolworths and get lamb; it's really good, you'll enjoy it', positions Woolworths as a site of quality and pleasure. However, Customer 1's insistence on Blacktown counters this, reaffirming halal authenticity. The juxtaposition with Woolworths, introduced by the shop-owner in line 9, does not serve to highlight halal availability but rather to emphasise quality. While there is some halal meat at Woolworths, the shop-owner's suggestion, 'You should go to Woolworths and get lamb; it's really good, you'll enjoy it', is not about competition between halal sources but about the quality of meat available there. In contrast, Customer 1's emphasis on Blacktown reflects a deeper investment in the authenticity of halal procurement, where trust in sourcing and religious compliance takes precedence over generalised notions of quality. This dynamic reflects what Scollon (2001) refers to as 'mediated action', where everyday practices, such as purchasing halal meat, are shaped by interactions with material conditions and social discourses (Shankar & Cavanaugh, 2017). This distinction underscores the ways in which food choices are not merely about taste but about the social and religious structures that shape perceptions of where and how food should be acquired (Ang, 2004). In this sense, the invocation of place is not merely about physical location but about trust and the perceived reliability of halal certification, embedded in the social networks that sustain it.

Incorporating Agha's (Agha, 2006, 2007a, 2007b) social theory of language strengthens this framework by emphasising that food choices, like language, are social semiotic resources. Agha (2007b, 2011) suggests that through language and food practices, individuals create reflexive models of behaviour, social groups, and social relations. As such, food practices, including halal consumption, are not just individual preferences but performative acts that mediate and construct larger social identities and relations. The linguistic and semiotic registers used in food discourse, such as 'halal' or 'authentic', function as vehicles for marking social distinctions and reinforcing normative models of behaviour. Agha's concept of enregisterment (2007a, b) is crucial here: the socially recognised categories of food, such as halal or non-halal, are products of collective evaluation and are tied to moral judgments about what is 'right' or 'wrong'. This theoretical lens clarifies how the interaction in Extract 10 is not just about food choices but about social positioning and the performance of cultural belonging within a diasporic context. Food becomes a signifier of identity, where halal certification and place are deeply entangled in the construction of moral and cultural values (Karrebæk, 2014).

Beyond questions of authentication, the discussion also foregrounds the role of taste and embodied memory in shaping diasporic food practices. Customer 1's observation in line 6 that 'The taste of the meat here is different from the taste of the meat in Iran' speaks to a broader discourse of authenticity, where taste is not simply a matter of individual preference but a socially mediated construct. In diasporic contexts, such remarks index a sensory dissonance that is not just about flavour but about the larger project of cultural reproduction in a new environment. The mention of 'the shank' introduces a specific culinary object, which is then validated through a social reference, Mahnaz and her guests, who 'loved it' and found it 'really delicious'. This transformation of an object into a socially endorsed commodity illustrates mediated action in which food is not merely consumed but co-constructed through discourse, relational networks, and affective connections. The act of purchasing, preparing, and evaluating meat becomes a mediated practice that extends beyond individual preference, supporting shared cultural knowledge and group belonging (Izadi, 2017, 2020, 2023). The mention of Mahnaz and her guests, who found it 'really delicious' in line 12, transforms the act of consumption into a communal and affective moment, aligning with the relational dimensions of food and the ways in which taste becomes a vehicle for sustaining cultural identity.

In line with Agha's (Agha, 2007a, 2007b) model, this mediation through taste and food practices demonstrates how food items are categorised (e.g., halal, delicious, healthy) in ways that carry moral judgments and social implications. Such categorisation mediates social relations, group belonging, and identity performance. In the context of halal meat, Customer 1's preference for Blacktown over Woolworths (a mainstream shop) shows that food choices are not only about taste but are deeply embedded in socio-cultural registers and semiotic performances. The invocation of place (Blacktown, Woolworths) functions as a marker of social models and normative behaviours, as Agha (2007a, 2007b) suggests, where the performance of halal consumption signals a particular social identity and adherence to cultural norms.

The interaction, although momentary and mundane, is not simply about the practicalities of purchasing halal meat but about the ways in which food choices are embedded in larger semiotic and social processes. The shop-owner's response, rather than deciding on what counts as 'authentic' halal, reflects a shared knowledge of the local halal landscape, where Blacktown is positioned as a trusted space of consumption. At the same time, the exchange reveals how indexicality operates in everyday discourse to organise perceptions of place, food, and belonging. The invocation of Blacktown and Woolworths signals a negotiation between different market spaces, each carrying distinct social meanings. Ultimately, this extract exemplifies how language, materiality, and semiotic resources interact in shaping everyday practices within diasporic communities. The conversation is not simply about meat but about broader negotiations of belonging, adaptation, and authenticity. Through discursive strategies, intertextual references, and spatial distinctions, the participants collectively construct a meaningful framework for making sense of their food choices in a new socio-cultural landscape. This highlights the role of language not merely as a communicative tool but as a dynamic medium through which cultural identities are continuously enacted and redefined.

Transitioning from the prior discussion of halal authenticity and sensory memory, the following interaction shifts focus to intercultural encounters and culinary exchange. In Extract 11, an Anglo-Australian female customer (C) who lives near the shop engages in a casual conversation with the shop-owner (SOW) and the researcher (R). As a frequent visitor, she often shares stories about how the shop-owners have introduced her to Persian cuisine, offering her food and teaching her how to cook it. This moment, unfolding in the quiet of the shop with no other customers present, creates an intimate setting where storytelling and cultural exchange take centre stage. Here, food is not just a marker of cultural identity but a bridge for cross-cultural learning, where shared narratives and embodied experiences shape perceptions of taste and authenticity.

Extract 11

1	C	My auntie made a what she calls a Persian rice like with a lot of spices and peanuts. It came from a Persian cook book
2	R	ah. OK
3	C	yeah but yeah so it's got sultana, lamb, its beautiful. It's actually although when I cooked it myself the first night wasn't that good and next day when all the spices and everything came out was beautiful, cinnamon and cardamom and all these beautiful spices in it.
4	SOW	but that rice
5	C	that
6	SOW	with a little bit of cinnamon.
7	C	does it yeah?
8	SOW	a little bit not much
9	C	She gave me some rice the other day, it was beautiful.

The customer's account of making Persian rice exemplifies what De Fina and Georgakopoulou (2015), describe as small stories, that is, everyday narratives that emerge in social interactions rather than fully structured, high-stakes storytelling events. Such narratives serve as sites of identity negotiation (De Fina, 2015) which allows the customer to position herself as someone engaging with Persian foodways (Di Giovine & Brulotte, 2016) while simultaneously reflecting on her own culinary experiences. By recounting her struggles and eventual success in making the dish, she positions herself as a learner, appropriating Persian culinary practices into her own repertoire. The storytelling process also involves entextualisation (Bauman & Briggs, 1990; Lempert & Perrino, 2007; Silverstein & Urban, 1996), that is, taking a recipe from a Persian cookbook (a mediated textual source), transferring it to her own kitchen, and recontextualising it within her personal experience. Through this process, Persian rice shifts from being a culturally embedded practice in its original setting to something that is reproduced and adapted in a new socio-cultural context. The Persian spices (cinnamon, cardamom, sultanas, in line 3) function as semiotic resources (van Leeuwen, 2005), indexing Persian culinary identity by evoking cultural associations and taste memories. However, these ingredients are more than just symbolic markers; they also serve as mediational tools (Norris & Jones, 2005; Scollon, 2001), actively shaping the enactment of Persian cuisine in a new context. In this interaction, the spices are not only material objects but also carriers of historical and social formations, which mediate between the cook, the dish, and its cultural significance. Their use demonstrates how material and symbolic dimensions intertwine in culinary practice, as the act of cooking itself becomes a site of cultural reproduction and transformation. Thus, the customer's engagement with the dish reflects a broader process of cultural negotiation, where both symbolic and material elements come together to shape her understanding and practice.

The shop-owner and the researcher (both knowledgeable due to their Persian background) also play key roles in authenticating the customer's experience with Persian food. In this context, the shop-owner's role becomes important in guiding the customer's engagement with Persian culinary practices. The shop-owner's brief interjection in line 4 ('but that rice') introduces a moment of cultural calibration, suggesting that the version of Persian rice the customer describes may not fully align with her own understanding of it. This is not a direct correction but an act of authentication, *gently* asserting a Persian perspective on how the dish should be recognised. The shop-owner's elaboration ('with a little bit of cinnamon' line 6) refines the customer's understanding, guiding her towards a more culturally validated version of the dish. The interaction (as illustrated in Extract 10) further emphasises the materiality of language in shaping cultural knowledge. It demonstrates how cultural knowledge is negotiated not only through spoken language but also through material objects, spices, cookbooks, and the act of cooking itself. The process of authentication is mediated by these objects, which function as both semiotic resources and mediational tools. Persian rice is not just verbally described but actively performed and reconfigured through the interplay of talk and materiality. Together, these elements contribute to the customer's evolving understanding of Persian cuisine, illustrating the dynamic interaction between identity, materiality, and cultural authenticity.

The shop-owner's act of cultural calibration in Extract 11 establishes the foundation for further cultural exchange, which unfolds in Extract 12. In line 10, the shop-owner shifts to Persian to name Adas Polo and با خرما وکشمش (with dates and raisins), but this is directed at the researcher, not the customer. This shift to Persian emphasises the cultural transmission that takes place between the shop-owner and the researcher, which strengthens the linguistic boundaries of the shop and positions the researcher as a participant in this cultural exchange. The use of Persian terms serves as a marker of cultural authenticity (Mapes, 2021), which draws attention to the shared insider knowledge. The shop-owner continues by naming Adas Polo and Qormeh Sabzi, embedding cultural materiality into the interaction. This naming process is a form of enregisterment, where these foods become indexed to Persian culinary tradition. By echoing these names, the researcher contributes to their semiotic mobility that is the ability of these food terms to transcend cultural contexts, as described by Silverstein (2003). Through repetition, these terms move beyond Persian cuisine and gain broader cultural recognition.

Extract 12

10	SOW	((turning to me saying)) Adas Polo ((in Persian she says)) با خرما و کشمش ((with dates and raisins)
11	R	oh Adas Polo
12	C	She gave me other foods.
13	SOW	Roast lamb ((laughing)).
14	C	what else did you give me? The thing with the beans in it, that was yummy.
15	SOW	(.) which one was it?
16	C	The red beans in it.
17	SOW	Oh yeah, Qormeh Sabzi.
18	R	Oh Qormeh Sabzi. That's one of my favourites.
19	C	That was yummy. Is it?
20	SOW	most of the Iranian favourite food.
21	R	Yes. That's right

The customer expresses appreciation for the dishes, particularly drawing attention to the flavours, which shows how food as a material object mediates social relationships between the shop-owner and the local community. This is significant because it reinforces the role of food not just as sustenance, but as a material entity that fosters community connection and cultural exchange. The laughter over roast lamb (line 13) further contrasts Persian and Anglo-Australian culinary traditions, offering an example of indexical contrast (Silverstein, 2021). This refers to how material objects, such as food, index or point to different cultural frames or traditions. In this case, the food item, roast lamb, serves as a point of comparison between the customer's potentially more familiar Anglo-Australian food practices and the Persian culinary traditions the shop-owner is introducing. The contrast between these two food practices highlights how food, as a semiotic object, can index both cultural differences and similarities, and serves as a tool for constructing identity in the context of these intercultural exchanges.

Extract 13 is a continuation of the interaction from Extracts 11 and 12, where the exchange between the customer, researcher, and shop-owner continues to explore the cultural dynamics of Persian food. In this section, the customer reflects upon the foods she has been given, including Tahdig, a Persian dish, which is introduced through a process of naming and pronunciation correction. In line 23, the shop-owner names 'kotlet' and other foods, while the customer expresses her admiration for the rice and describes it in detail, leading to a discussion about Tahdig. The interaction becomes centred around language materiality, as the act of naming and pronouncing 'Tahdig' emphasises how linguistic forms are mediated through material engagement (Manning, 2012). The customer's sensory experience of eating the dish, for example, its taste, appearance, and texture, becomes intertwined with the process of learning its name. This relationship between the linguistic and sensory experience underscores how language can be embodied through interaction.

Extract 13

22	C	and there was also (((thinking about the other food SOW gave her)) um . . . oh heaps of stuff that she's giving me beautiful food
23	SOW	kotlet
24	C	I love the rice. It's the best rice I had in my life.
25	R	the rice?
26	C	yes, the long grain that's really skinny, beautiful rice and the bottom was so sticky.
27	R	down the bottom you mean?
28	C	Yeah I loved that. And the bread on the bottom.
29	R	it's called Tahdig. at the bottom

30	SOW	Tahdig
31	C	((trying to pronounce like me and SOW)) Tahdig
32	SOW	TahDIG ((SOW is teaching her how to say it correctly))
33	C	TahDIG ((saying like SOW)). I'll probably forget it
34	R	((I'm trying to sound it out for her)) Tah
35	C	Tah
36	R	Dig
37	C	Dig
38	C	Tahdig ((saying it perfectly))
39	R	meaning at the bottom of the dish
40	C	yeah, yeah it's beautiful.

In the structured repetition of 'Tahdig' (Turns 31–38), the shop-owner's phonetic correction (Turn 32) and the researcher's breakdown of syllables (Turns 34–37) exemplify the collaborative nature of enregisterment. Here, language learning is not just a cognitive process, but it is actively shaped through multisensory engagement (sound, touch, and taste). Teaching the correct pronunciation of 'Tahdig' is not just a matter of phonetic correction but a shared, embodied practice that connects the customer's newfound knowledge with the materiality of the food itself. The customer's comment, 'I'll probably forget it' (Turn 33), followed by her eventual correct pronunciation in line 38, signals a moment of enregisterment. This process of acquiring and attempting to retain a Persian term shows how unfamiliar terms are gradually integrated into the speaker's repertoire, even if temporarily. The final turns (39–40) further reinforce the indexical meaning (Silverstein, 2021) of 'Tahdig', as it is anchored in Persian culinary traditions. The explanation of its meaning (at the bottom of the dish in line 29) frames the dish through a spatial metaphor, reinforcing its connection to Persian food culture and its materiality within that context.

In these extracts, the customer, researcher, and shop-owner engage in an exchange about Persian food, with the shop-owner introducing dishes like Adas Polo and Qormeh Sabzi and guiding the customer through the pronunciation of Tahdig. Through collaborative naming, repetition, and sensory experiences, food and language work together to mediate cultural knowledge (Appadurai, 2015; Scollon, 2001) and reinforce the customer's connection to Persian culinary traditions.

6 Conclusion

In this Element, I explore the intersections of language, materiality, and cultural identity within diasporic contexts, specifically focusing on how imported Persian ingredients and everyday items – which are often found in mainstream supermarkets in Australia such as Coles and Woolworths – serve as cultural symbols and mediators of social encounters. The study moves beyond food itself, examining conversations about these items to understand their role in negotiating identity and authenticity in a multicultural marketplace. Drawing on interdisciplinary theories from social semiotics (van Leeuwen, 2005), multimodal communication, and linguistic anthropology, this Element integrates frameworks that emphasise the materiality of objects in shaping social dynamics. Latour's concept of actants helps frame the role of objects as active participants in these interactions, while Miller's materiality provides a lens for understanding how objects carry cultural significance and influence social relationships. Appadurai's theory of mediation highlights how these objects circulate across cultural boundaries, affecting how identity is constructed and performed. Scollon's mediational means theory further enriches the analysis by emphasising how both language and material objects work together to facilitate social interaction. In addition, Shankar and Cavanaugh's perspectives on language and materiality contribute to understanding the fluid and context-dependent nature of these negotiations. Methodologically, through an ethnographic methodology, including participant observation and conversation analysis, this Element delves into everyday interactions between customers and shop-owners, demonstrating how objects mediate social relationships and contribute to the negotiation of cultural identity.

The findings underscore the critical role of objects in mediating cultural exchanges, highlighting not only the food itself but also the conversations and cultural understanding these discussions facilitate. Objects such as Persian ingredients, fruit dates, legal documents like powers of attorney, and symbols on shop signs emerged as active *mediators* of cultural values and legal frameworks within the diasporic space. For instance, the power of attorney (in Extract 3), as a legal document, functioned as an actant, representing the landowner who resides in Australia but is unable to return to Iran to sell the land. This document, through its legal significance, symbolised a complex intersection of cultural and legal practices. These objects were not passive; instead, they actively facilitated learning for non-Persian customers, transforming the shop into a cultural transmitter and educational space for engagement and exchange. In Extracts 11–13, for example, Anglo-Australian customers not only learned about Persian food but also practised pronouncing its names, illustrating how food-related objects in the shop became sites for cultural education. Similarly, dates, a staple in Persian cuisine (as discussed in Extracts 6 and 7), were viewed differently by customers based on their cultural backgrounds. Anglo-Australian customers, unfamiliar with the varieties of Persian dates, expressed curiosity and appreciation for their distinctive taste and appearance. In contrast, Persian-speaking customers focused more on the cultural significance and traditional uses of the fruit. For the shop-owner, dates were not merely a commodity but an emblem of cultural authenticity, connecting heritage with the diasporic community. The shop thus served as a dynamic site where linguistic practices and material objects coalesced, encouraging the negotiation of cultural identity. As a place of engagement, it fostered cultural learning through interactions that integrated language, food, and objects, allowing customers to explore and understand Persian food practices and identity. Such encounters illustrate the intertwined nature of language, materiality, and cultural understanding in constructing authenticity within a multicultural marketplace.

The findings move beyond viewing objects as static cultural markers and instead accentuate instead their broader role as active mediators of cultural exchange. They demonstrate that objects such as food, documents, and other material items are central to the dynamics of cultural engagement. Through examining the ways in which objects are discussed, handled, and perceived, the study brings to the fore how they play a crucial role in identity negotiation and cultural learning. It is not merely the food items themselves but the conversations surrounding these objects, as well as the habitual practices and interpretations attached to them, that shape and are shaped by people's lives. This process of cultural exchange is deeply tied to objects, their materiality, and the meanings we attribute to them. This aligns with recent work in material culture and cultural studies (e.g., Appadurai, 1986; Manning, 2012; Miller, 2005; Shankar & Cavanaugh, 2017), which demonstrates the significant role of objects in mediating social relations and the transmission of cultural knowledge. By focusing on the semiotics of objects in intercultural contexts, this research contributes to a deeper understanding of how objects act as powerful agents in the negotiation of identity and cultural authenticity.

These findings are important because they offer practical insights into how everyday interactions in multicultural spaces can be more inclusive and culturally responsive. For instance, educators, community workers, and intercultural trainers could use the examples from this study to design activities that highlight the role of material culture in facilitating understanding across cultural boundaries. Such activities might include role-plays or scenario-based discussions where participants engage with culturally significant objects, fostering empathy and awareness of diverse worldviews. Retailers or cultural centres might also rethink how they display or narrate products from different traditions to promote meaningful engagement rather than tokenism. This could involve curating stories and contexts behind products, engaging community voices in the curation process, and encouraging dialogue between customers and staff about the cultural significance of items. By grounding these efforts in real-world interactions, stakeholders can foster deeper intercultural understanding and appreciation.

While the study provides valuable insights into the role of objects in cultural exchange, a few limitations should be noted. First, the research was conducted within a single ethnic shop, which may limit the broader applicability of the findings to other communities or contexts. Moreover, the focus on verbal and material semiotics, while central to understanding the mediation of culture, did not fully encompass the sensory and embodied experiences that could further illuminate the role of food, for instance, in these exchanges. In addition, the absence of in-depth interviews limits the ability to capture participants' reflections on these experiences. Future studies could incorporate interviews with shopkeepers and customers to gain deeper insight into their motivations, memories, and identity negotiations. Such narratives would provide richer accounts of how individuals interpret their interactions with material objects and allow researchers to trace the affective and historical dimensions embedded in everyday encounters. To build on these findings, future research could expand the scope to include diverse diasporic communities and explore the multisensory dimensions of food interactions. Further studies could also investigate the role of social media and digital platforms in the spread of culinary practices in globalised contexts, considering how online spaces facilitate intercultural exchanges. In addition, exploring the socio-political aspects of food consumption such as the influence of race, class, and migration status could deepen our understanding of how cultural identities are negotiated and represented within diasporic communities. This expansion could also uncover the structural conditions that shape access to cultural representation and authenticity.

In conclusion, this research contributes to a more nuanced understanding of how material objects, language, and materiality interact to shape cultural identities in diasporic settings. By exploring the dynamic processes through which objects mediate cultural exchange and authenticity, the study opens up avenues for further research into the complex entanglements of materiality, language, and identity in globalised contexts. Practitioners and researchers interested in intercultural communication, education, or migration studies can apply these insights to support cultural learning, develop inclusive policies, and foreground material practices in their analyses. This focus on material-discursive practices can help shift policy frameworks beyond abstract notions of diversity, anchoring them in the everyday realities and interactions of diasporic life. Ultimately, such an approach emphasises the importance of studying the mundane and the material as vital sites for understanding social change, belonging, and identity. Future investigations could build on these findings to develop a more comprehensive understanding of how objects, as material and semiotic entities, facilitate the negotiation of authenticity and belonging in diasporic communities.

References

Adamiyat, F. (1354/1975). *Amir Kabir va Iran* (4th ed.). Intisharat-i Kharazmi.

Adekunle, B., & Filson, G. (2020). Understanding halal food market: Resolving asymmetric information. *Food Ethics*, *5*(1–2), 1–22. https://doi.org/10.1007/s41055-020-00072-7.

Agar, M. H. (1997). Ethnography: An overview. *Substance Use & Misuse*, *32*(9), 1155–1173. https://doi.org/10.3109/10826089709035470.

Agha, A. (2006). *Language and social relations*. Cambridge University Press.

Agha, A. (2007a). The object called 'language' and the subject of linguistics. *Journal of English Linguistics*, *35*(3), 217–235. https://doi.org/10.1177/0075424207304240.

Agha, A. (2007b). Recombinant selves in mass mediated spacetime. *Language & Communication*, *27*(3), 320–335. https://doi.org/10.1016/j.langcom.2007.01.001.

Agha, A. (2011). Meet mediatization. Language & communication, 31(3), 163–170.https://doi.org/10.1016/j.langcom.2011.03.006.

Ahmed, S. (2014). *The cultural politics of emotion* (4th ed.). Routledge

Ang, I. (2004). Between Asia and the West: The cultural politics of food. *Life Writing*, *1*(1), 147–153. www.tandfonline.com/action/showCitFormats?doi=10.1080/10408340308518248.

Appadurai, A. (1986). Introduction: Commodities and the politics of value. In A. Appadurai (Ed.), *The social life of things: Commodities in cultural perspective* (pp. 3–63). Cambridge University Press.

Appadurai, A. (1996). *Modernity at large: Cultural dimensions of globalization*. University of Minnesota Press.

Appadurai, A. (2015). Mediants, materiality, normativity. *Public Culture*, *27*(2), 221–237. https://doi.org/10.1215/08992363-2841832.

Aronin, L., & Ó Laoire, M. (2013). The material culture of multilingualism: Moving beyond the linguistic landscape. *International Journal of Multilingualism*, *10*(3), 225–235. https://doi.org/10.1080/14790718.2012.679734.

Auger, N., & Dervin, F. (2021). Special issue: A discourse toolbox for working on interculturality in education. *International Journal of Bias, Identity and Diversities in Education (IJBIDE)*, *1*(6), vi–x.

Austin, J. L. (1962). *How to do things with words*. Oxford University Press.

Badwan, K., & Hall, E. (2020). Walking along in sticky places: Post-humanist and affective insights from a reflective account of two young women in

Manchester, UK. *Language and Intercultural Communication, 20*(3), 225–239. https://doi.org/10.1080/14708477.2020.1715995.

Australian Bureau of Statistics. (2021). Retrieved February 20, 2025, from http://www.abs.gov.au.

Bailey, B. (2000). Communicative behavior and conflict between African-American customers and Korean immigrant retailers in Los Angeles. *Discourse & Society*, 11(1), 86–108. https://doi.org/10.1177/0957926500011001004

Bakhtin, M. (1982). *The dialogic imagination: Four essays* (Trans. C. Emerson & M. Holquist ; Ed. M. Holquist). University of Texas Press.

Barad, K. (2003). Posthumanist performativity: Toward an understanding of how matter comes to matter. *Signs: Journal of Women in Culture and Society, 28*(3), 801–831. www.jstor.org/stable/10.1086/345321.

Barnes, A. (2017). Telling stories: The role of graphic design and branding in the creation of 'authenticity' within food packaging. *International Journal of Food Design, 2*(2), 183–202. https://doi.org/10.1386/ijfd.2.2.183_1.

Bauman, R., & Briggs, C. L. (1990). Poetics and performance as critical perspectives on language and social life. *Annual Review of Anthropology, 19*, 59–88. www.jstor.org/stable/2155959.

Bennett, J. (2010). *Vibrant matter: A political ecology of things*. Duke University Press.

Benso, S. (2000). *The face of things: A different side of ethics*. State University of New York Press.

Blackledge, A., & Creese, A. (2017). Translanguaging and the body. *International Journal of Multilingualism, 14*(3), 250–268. https://doi.org/10.1080/14790718.2017.1315809.

Blommaert, J. (2005). *Discourse: A critical introduction*. Cambridge University Press.

Blommaert, J. (2010). *The sociolinguistics of globalization*. Cambridge University Press.

Blommaert, J., & Backus, A. (2013). Superdiverse repertoires and the individual. In I. d. Saint-Georges & J.-J. Weber (Eds.), *Multilingualism and multimodality: Current challenges for educational studies* (pp. 9–32). Brill.

Blommaert, J. & De Fina, A. (2017). Chronotopic identities: On the spacetime organization of who we are. In A. De Fina, D. Ikizoglu and J. Wegner (eds) *Diversity and Superdiversity: Sociocultural Linguistic Perspectives* (pp. 1–15). Washington: Georgetown University Press.

Bourdieu, P. (1977a). Cultural reproduction and social reproduction. In J. Karabel & A. H. Halsey (Eds.), *Power and ideology in education* (pp. 487–511). Oxford University Press.

Bourdieu, P. (1977b). *Outline of a theory of practice*. Cambridge University Press.

Bourdieu, P. (1985). *Distinction: A social critique of the judgement of taste*. Harvard University Press.

Bucholtz, M., & Hall, K. (2005). Identity and interaction: A sociocultural linguistic approach. *Discourse Studies*, *7*(4–5), 585–614.

Bucholtz, M., & Hall, K. (2016). Embodied sociolinguistics. In N. Coupland (Ed.), *Sociolinguistics: Theoretical debates* (pp. 173–197). Cambridge University Press.

Callon, M. (1984). Some elements of a sociology of translation: Domestication of the Scallops and the Fishermen of St Brieuc Bay. *The Sociological Review*, *32*(1), 196–233. https://doi.org/10.1111/j.1467-954X.1984.tb00113.x.

Callon, M. (1991). Techno-economic networks and irreversibility. In L. John (Ed.), *A Sociology of monsters: Essays on power, technology and domination* (pp. 132–161). Routledge.

Callon, M. (1999). Actor-network theory – the market test. *The Sociological Review*, *47*(S1), 181–195. https://doi.org/10.1111/j.1467-954X.1999.tb03488.x.

Callon, M., & Latour, B. (1981). Unscrewing the big leviathan: How actors macro-structure reality and how sociologists help them to do so. In K. K. Cetina & A. V. Cicourel (Eds.), *Advances in social theory and methodology: Towards an integration of micro-and macro-sociologies* (pp. 277–303). Routledge.

Callon, M., & Muniesa, F. (2005). Peripheral vision: Economic markets as calculative collective devices. *Organization Studies*, *26*(8), 1229–1250. https://doi.org/10.1177/0170840605056393.

Canagarajah, S. (2018). Translingual practice as spatial repertoires: Expanding the paradigm beyond structuralist orientations. *Applied Linguistics*, *39*(1), 31–54. https://doi.org/10.1093/applin/amx041.

Caron, A. H., & Caronia, L. (2007). *Moving cultures: Mobile communication in everyday life*. McGill-Queen's Press-MQUP.

Caronia, L., & Cooren, F. (2014). Decentering our analytical position: The dialogicity of things. *Discourse & Communication*, *8*(1), 41–61. https://doi.org/10.1177/1750481313503226.

Cavanaugh, J. R. (2007). Making salami, producing Bergamo: The transformation of value. *Ethnos*, *72*(2), 149–172. https://doi.org/10.1080/00141840701387853.

Cavanaugh, J. R., & Shankar, S. (2014). Producing authenticity in global capitalism: Language, materiality, and value. *American Anthropologist*, *116*(1), 51–64. https://doi.org/10.1111/aman.12075.

Cerulo, K. A. (2009). Nonhumans in social interaction. *Annual Review of Sociology*, *35*(1), 531–552. https://doi.org/10.1146/annurev-soc-070308-120008.

Cerulo, K. A. (2011). Social interaction: Do non-humans count? *Sociology Compass*, *5*(9), 775–791. https://doi.org/10.1111/j.1751-9020.2011.00404.x.

Coole, D., & Frost, S. (2010). *New materialisms: Ontology, agency, and politics*. Duke University Press.

Cooren, F. (2004). Textual agency: How texts do things in organizational settings. Organization, 11(3), 373–393. https://doi.org/10.1177/1350508404041998.

Cornips, L. (2024). The semiotic repertoire of dairy cows. *Language in Society*, 1–25. https://doi.org/10.1017/S0047404524000460.

Cornips, L., & van Koppen, M. (2024). Multimodal dairy cow–human interaction in an intensive farming context. *Language Sciences*, *101*, 1–14. https://doi.org/10.1016/j.langsci.2023.101587.

Daston, L. (2004). Introduction: Speechless. In L. Daston (Ed.), *Things that talk: Object lessons from art and science* (pp. 9–24). Princeton University Press.

De Fina, A. (2015). Narrative and identities. In A. De Fina & A. Georgakopoulou (Eds.), *The handbook of narrative analysis* (pp. 349–368). Wiley.

De Fina, A., & Georgakopoulou, A. (2015). Introduction. In A. De Fina & A. Georgakopoulou (Eds.), *The handbook of narrative analysis* (pp. 1–17). Wiley.

Deleuze, G., & Guattari, F. L. (1987). A thousand plateaus: Capitalism and schizophrenia (B. Massumi, Trans.). Minneapolis, MN: University of Minnesota Press.

Di Giovine, M. A., & Brulotte, R. L. (2016). Introduction food and foodways as cultural heritage. In R. L. Brulotte & M. A. D. Giovine (Eds.), *Edible identities: Food as cultural heritage* (pp. 1–27). Routledge.

Doane, J., & Hodges, D. (1987). *Nostalgia and sexual difference: The resistance to contemporary feminism*. Routledge.

Douglas, M. (2002). *Purity and danger: An analysis of concepts of pollution and taboo*. Routledge Classics.

Dovchin, S. (2021). Translanguaging, emotionality, and English as a second language immigrants: Mongolian background women in Australia. *Tesol Quarterly*, *55*(3), 839–865. https://doi.org/10.1002/tesq.3015.

Duranti, A. (1997). *Linguistic anthropology*. Cambridge University Press.

Elabdali, R. (2024). Yalla Nutbikh 'Let's Cook': Negotiating emotions of belonging through food in heritage language classrooms. *Modern Language Journal*, *108*(S1), 56–74. https://doi.org/10.1111/modl.12901.

Garfinkel, H. (1967). *Studies in ethnomethodology*. Prentice-Hall.

Geertz, C. (1973). *The interpretation of cultures: Selected essays.* Basic Books.

Gell, A. (1998). *Art and agency: An anthropological theory.* Oxford University Press.

Goffman, E. (1959). The presentation of self in everyday life. London: Anchor Books.

Goffman, E. (1974). *Frame analysis: An essay on the organization of experience.* Northeastern University.

Gombrich, E. H. (1979). *The sense of order: A study in the psychology of decorative art.* Phaidon Press.

Gosden, C., & Marshall, Y. (1999). The cultural biography of objects. *World Archaeology, 31*(2), 169–178. https://doi.org/10.1080/00438243.1999.9980439.

Gumperz, J. (1964). Linguistic and social interaction in two communities. *American Anthropologist, 66*(6), 137–153. www.jstor.org/stable/668168.

Gumperz, J. (1971). *Language in social groups.* Stanford University Press.

Gumperz, J. (2015). Interactional sociolinguistics: A personal perspective. In D. Tannen, H. E. Hamilton, & D. Schiffrin (Eds.), *The handbook of discourse analysis* (pp. 309–323). John Wiley & Sons.

Hammersley, M., & Atkinson, P. (2019). *Ethnography: Principles in practice* (4th ed.). Routledge.

Harkness, N. (2015). The pragmatics of qualia in practice. *Annual Review of Anthropology, 44*(1), 573–589.

Harvey, D. (1990). Between space and time: Reflections on the geographical imagination. *Annals of the Association of American Geographers, 80*(3), 418–434. https://doi.org/10.1111/j.1467-8306.1990.tb00305.x.

Hegel, G. (1977). *Phenomenology of spirit.* Oxford University Press.

Henare, A., Holbraad, M., & Wastell, S. (Eds.). (2007). *Thinking through things: Theorising artefacts ethnographically.* Routledge.

Hopkyns, S. (2025). Sticky objects and places: Entangled emotions in an English-Medium university educationscape. *International Journal of Applied Linguistics, 35*(3), 1019–1030. https://doi.org/10.1111/ijal.12704.

Hoskins, J. (2006). Agency, biography and objects. In C. Tilley, W. Keane, S. Kuechler, M. Rowlands, & P. Spyer (Eds.), *Handbook of material culture* (pp. 74–84). Sage.

Izadi, D. (2015). Spatial engagement in Persian ethnic shops in Sydney. *Multimodal Communication, 4*(1), 61–78. https://doi.org/10.1515/mc-2015-0005.

Izadi, D. (2017). Semiotic resources and mediational tools in Merrylands, Sydney, Australia: The case of Persian and Afghan shops. *Social Semiotics, 27*(4), 495–512. https://doi.org/10.1080/10350330.2017.1334401.

Izadi, D. (2019). 'Are these ones to taste?': Critical moments in Persian shops in Sydney. In S. H. Mirvahedi (Ed.), *The sociolinguistics of Iran's languages at home and abroad: The case of Persian, Azerbaijani, and Kurdish* (pp. 169–196). Palgrave Macmillan.

Izadi, D. (2020). *The spatial and temporal dimensions of interactions*. Palgrave Macmillan.

Izadi, D. (2023). Exploring the phenomenology of shopping as social practice: An inquiry into the multimodal and linguistic repertoires in markets in Sydney. In G. Rasmussen & T. v. Leeuwen (Eds.), *Multimodality and social interaction in online and offline shopping* (pp. 13–39). Routledge.

Izadi, D., & Luke, A. (2025). Dialogues of materiality: Unravelling the agency of discourse and objects. *Multimodal Communication*, *14*(1), 1–16. https://doi.org/10.1515/mc-2024-0105.

Izadi, D., & Parvaresh, V. (2016). The framing of the linguistic landscapes of Persian shop signs in Sydney. *Linguistic Landscape*, *2*(2), 182–205. https://doi.org/10.1075/ll.2.2.04iza.

Järlehed, J., Milani, T. M., & Rosendal, T. (2023). Introducing the political economy of language in place/space. *Linguistic Landscape*, *9*(3), 219–225. https://doi.org/10.1075/ll.23039.jar.

Järlehed, J., & Moriarty, M. (2018). Culture and class in a glass: Scaling the semiofoodscape. *Language & Communication*, *62*, 26–38. https://doi.org/10.1016/j.langcom.2018.05.003.

Jaworski, A. (2015). Word cities and language objects: 'Love' sculptures and signs as shifter. *Linguistic Landscape*, *1*(1/2), 75–94. https://doi.org/10.1075/ll.1.1-2.05jaw.

Jaworski, A., & Thurlow, C. (2010). Introducing semiotic landscapes. In A. Jaworski & C. Thurlow(Eds.), Semiotic landscapes: Language, image, space (pp. 1–40). London: Continuum.

Jocuns, A., & Groot, F. O. d. (2025). Geographies of discourse revisited. *Multimodal Communication*, *14*(1), 23–36. https://doi.org/10.1515/mc-2024-0112.

Johnston, J., & Baumann, S. (2014). *Foodies: Democracy and distinction in the gourmet foodscape* (2nd ed.). Routledge.

Johnstone, B. (2004). Place, globalization, and linguistic variation. In C. Fought (Ed.), *Sociolinguistic variation: Critical reflections* (pp. 65–83). Oxford University Press.

Karimzad, F., & Catedral, L. (2021). *Chronotopes and migration: Language, social imagination, and behavior*. Routledge.

Karrebæk, M. S. (2014). Rye bread and halal: Enregisterment of food practices in the primary classroom. *Language & Communication, 34*, 17–34. https://doi.org/10.1016/j.langcom.2013.08.002.

Karrebæk, M. S., & Maegaard, M. (2024). The language of smoked fish: The production and circulation of meanings and values of 'Bornholmian Food'. *Language in Society, 54*(1), 1–29. https://doi.org/10.1017/S004740452400068X.

Keane, W. (2001). Money is no object: Materiality, desire, and modernity in an Indonesian society. In F. R. Myers (Ed.), *The empire of things: Regimes of value and material culture* (pp. 65–90). School of American Research.

Keane, W. (2003). Semiotics and the social analysis of material things. *Language & Communication, 23*(3–4), 409–425. https://doi.org/10.1016/S0271-5309(03)00010-7.

Kebabi, A. (2024). 'Identity' is not only about human relations: The relevance of human-to-non-human interaction in 'identity' articulation. *Language and Intercultural Communication, 24*(1), 6–19. https://doi.org/10.1080/14708477.2023.2252779.

Kopytoff, I. (1986). The cultural biography of things: Commoditization as process. In A. Appadurai (Ed.), *The social life of things: Commodities in cultural perspective* (pp. 64–91). Cambridge University Press.

Lamb, G., & Higgins, C. (2020). Posthumanism and its implications for discourse studies. In A. D. Fina & A. Georgakopoulou (Eds.), *The Cambridge handbook of discourse studies* (pp. 350–370). Cambridge University Press.

Latour, B. (1987). *Science in action: How to follow scientists and engineers through society.* Cambridge.

Latour, B. (1992). Where are the missing masses? The sociology of a few mundane artifacts. In J. Law & W. E. Bijker (Eds.), *Shaping technology/building Society: Studies in sociotechnical change* (pp. 225–258). The MIT Press.

Latour, B. (1993). *We have never been modern (trans. C. Porter).* Cambridge.

Latour, B. (1996a). On actor-network theory: A few clarifications. *Soziale welt, 47*(4), 369–381. www.jstor.org/stable/40878163.

Latour, B. (1996b). On interobjectivity. *Mind, Culture, and Activity, 3*(4), 228–245. https://doi.org/10.1207/s15327884mca0304_2.

Latour, B. (1996c). Pursuing the discussion of interobjectivity with a few friends. *Mind, Culture, and Activity, 3*(4), 266–269. https://doi.org/10.1207/s15327884mca0304_6.

Latour, B. (1999). *Pandora's hope: Essays on the reality of science studies.* Cambridge.

Latour, B. (2005). *Reassembling the social: An introduction to actor-network-theory*. Oxford University Press.

Latour, B., & Venn, C. (2002). Morality and technology. *Theory, Culture & Society, 19*(5–6), 247–260.

Latour, B., & Woolgar, S. (1986). *Laboratory life: The construction of scientific facts*. Princeton University Press.

Law, J. (1987). Technology and heterogeneous engineering: The case of Portuguese expansion. In W. E. Bijker, T. P. Hughes, & T. Pinch (Eds.), *The social construction of technological: New directions in the sociology and history of technology studies* (pp. 111–134). The MIT Press.

Lempert, M., & Perrino, S. (2007). Entextualization and the ends of temporality. *Language & Communication, 27*(3), 205–211. https://doi.org/10.1016/j.langcom.2007.01.005.

Lou, J. J. (2016). Shop sign as monument: The discursive recontextualization of a neon sign. *Linguistic Landscape: An International Journal, 2*(3), 211–222. https://doi.org/10.1075/ll.2.3.01lou.

Lou, J. J. (2017). Spaces of consumption and senses of place: A geosemiotic analysis of three markets in Hong Kong. *Social Semiotics, 27*(4), 513–531. https://doi.org/10.1080/10350330.2017.1334403.

Maguire, J. S. (2016). Looking at food practices and taste across the class divide. *Food, Culture & Society, 19*(1), 11–18. https://doi.org/10.1080/15528014.2016.1144995.

Manning, P. (2012). *Semiotics of drink and drinking*. Continuum.

Manning, P. (2017). The semiotic ecology of drinks and talk in Georgia. In J. R. Cavanaugh & S. Shankar (Eds.), *Language and materiality: Ethnographic and theoretical explorations* (pp. 226–247). Cambridge University Press.

Mapes, G. (2021). *Elite authenticity: Remaking distinction in food discourse*. Oxford University.

Matthee, R. (1996). From coffee to tea: Shifting patterns of consumption in Qajar Iran. *Journal of World History, 7*(2), 199–230. www.jstor.org/stable/20078676.

Miller, D. (2005). Materiality: An introduction. In D. Miller (Ed.), *Materiality* (pp. 1–50). Duke University Press.

Mondada, L. (2016). Challenges of multimodality: Language and the body in social interaction. *Journal of Sociolinguistics, 20*(3), 336–366. https://doi.org/10.1111/josl.1_12177.

Mondada, L. (2018). The multimodal interactional organization of tasting: Practices of tasting cheese in gourmet shops. *Discourse Studies, 20*(6), 743–769. https://doi.org/10.1177/1461445618793439.

Noble, G. (2002). Comfortable and relaxed: Furnishing the home and nation. *Continuum: Journal of Media & Cultural Studies*, *16*(1), 53–66. https://doi.org/10.1080/10304310220120975.

Noble, G. (2004). Accumulating being. *International Journal of Cultural Studies*, *7*(2), 233–256. https://doi.org/10.1177/1367877904043239.

Norris, S. (2004). *Analyzing multimodal interaction: A methodological framework*. Routledge.

Norris, S. (2011). *Identity in (inter)action: Introducing multimodal (inter)action*. de Gruyter Mouton.

Norris, S., & Jones, R. H. (Eds.). (2005). *Discourse in action: Introducing mediated discourse analysis*. Routledge.

Peirce, C. S. (1995). *Philosophical writings of Peirce*. Dover.

Pennycook, A. (2017). Translanguaging and semiotic assemblages. *International Journal of Multilingualism*, *14*(3), 269–282. https://doi.org/10.1080/14790718.2017.1315810.

Pennycook, A. (2018a). *Posthumanist applied linguistics*. Routledge.

Pennycook, A. (2018b). Posthumanist applied linguistics. *Applied Linguistics*, *39*(4), 445–461. https://doi.org/10.1093/applin/amw016.

Pennycook, A., & Otsuji, E. (2015). Making scents of the landscape. *Linguistic Landscape*, *1*(3), 191–212. https://doi.org/10.1075/ll.1.3.01pen

Pietikäinen, S., & Hegel, C. (2021). Assembling success: Desire, worker mobility, and value creation in Finnish ice hockey. *Anthropology of Work Review*, *42*(2), 71–81. https://doi.org/10.1111/awr.12221.

Pietikäinen, S., Jaffe, A., Kelly-Holmes, H., & Coupland, N. (2016). *Sociolinguistics from the periphery: Small languages in new circumstances*. Cambridge University Press.

Rampton, B. (2007). Neo-Hymesian linguistic ethnography in the United Kingdom. *Journal of Sociolinguistics*, *11*(5), 584–607. https://doi.org/10.1111/j.1467-9841.2007.00341.x.

Riley, K., & Cavanaugh, J. (2017). Tasty talk, expressive food: An introduction to the semiotics of food and language. *Semiotic Review Online*, *5*. https://doi.org/https:==www.semioticreview.com=ojs=index.php=sr=article=view=1.

Ros i Solé, C. (2025). *Material interculturality: Making sense with everyday objects*. Routledge.

Rymes, B. (2010). Classroom discourse analysis: A focus on communicative repertoires. In N. H. Hornberger & S. L. McKay (Eds.), *Sociolinguistics and language education* (pp. 528–546). Multilingual Matters.

Sacks, H. (1992). *Lectures on conversation, vols. 1 and 2*. Blackwell.

Sarangi, S. (2007). The anatomy of interpretation: Coming to terms with the analyst's paradox in professional discourse studies. *Text & Talk, 27*(5–6), 567–584. https://doi.org/10.1515/TEXT.2007.025.

Saurma-Jeltsch, L. E. (2010). About the agency of things, of objects and artefacts. In d. L. E. Saurma-Jeltsch & A. Eisenbeiß (Eds.), *The power of things and the flow of cultural transformations* (pp. 10–22). Deutscher Kunstverlag.

Sayes, E. (2012). From the sacred to the sacred object: Girard, Serres, and Latour on the ordering of the human collective. *Techne: Research in Philosophy & Technology, 16*(2). https://doi.org/10.5840/techne201216211.

Sayes, E. (2014). Actor–Network Theory and methodology: Just what does it mean to say that nonhumans have agency? *Social Studies of Science, 44*(1), 134–149. https://doi.org/10.1177/0306312713511867.

Scollon, R. (2001). *Mediated discourse: The nexus of practice.* Routledge.

Scollon, R. (2013). Geographies of discourse: Action across layered spaces. In I. D. Saint-Georges & J.-J. Weber (Eds.), *Multilingualism and multimodality: Current challenges for educational studies* (pp. 183–198). Sense.

Scollon, R., & Scollon, S. W. (2003). *Discourses in place: Language in the material world.* Routledge.

Scollon, R. & Scollon, S. W. (2004). *Nexus analysis: Discourse and the emerging internet.* Routledge.

Shankar, S. (2006). Metaconsumptive practices and the circulation of objectifications. *Journal of Material Culture, 11*(3), 293–317. https://doi.org/10.1177/1359183506068807.

Shankar, S., & Cavanaugh, J. R. (2012). Language and materiality in global capitalism. *Annual Review of Anthropology, 41*(1), 355–369. https://doi.org/10.1146/annurev-anthro-092611-145811.

Shankar, S., & Cavanaugh, J. R. (2017). Toward a theory of language materiality: An introduction. In S. Shankar & J. R. Cavanaugh (Eds.), *Language and materiality: Ethnographic and theoretical explorations* (pp. 1–28). Cambridge University Press.

Silverstein, M. (2003). Indexical order and the dialectics of sociolinguistic life. *Language & Communication, 23*(3–4), 193–229. https://doi.org/10.1016/S0271-5309(03)00013-2.

Silverstein, M. (2021). The dialectics of indexical semiosis: Scaling up and out from the 'actual' to the 'virtual'. *International Journal of the Sociology of Language 21*(272), 13–45. https://doi.org/10.1515/ijsl-2021-2124.

Silverstein, M., & Urban, G. (Eds.). (1996). *Natural histories of discourse.* The University of Chicago Press.

Tannock, S. (1995). Nostalgia critique. *Cultural Studies*, *9*(3), 453–464. https://doi.org/10.1080/09502389500490511.

Thurlow, C. (2016). Queering critical discourse studies or/and performing 'post-class' ideologies. *Critical Discourse Studies*, *13*(5), 485–514. https://doi.org/10.1080/17405904.2015.1122646.

Thurlow, C. (2020). Expanding our sociolinguistic horizons? Geographical thinking and the articulatory potential of commodity chain analysis. *Journal of Sociolinguistics*, *24*(3), 350–368. https://doi.org/10.1111/josl.12388.

van Leeuwen, T. (2005). *Introducing social semiotics: An introductory textbook*. Routledge.

Wertsch, J. V. (1998). *Mind as action*. Oxford University Press.

Zhu, H., Wei, L., & Lyons, A. (2017). Polish shop (ping) as translanguaging space. *Social Semiotics*, *27*(4), 411–433. https://doi.org/10.1080/10350330.2017.1334390.

Acknowledgements

My sincere thanks to Zhu Hua and Li Wei, editors of Cambridge Elements in Applied Linguistics, for their generous support and intellectual leadership throughout the development of this work. I am especially grateful to Zhu Hua for her support and constructive feedback at every stage of the process. I also wish to thank the anonymous reviewers whose insightful comments greatly shaped the final version of this Element. Their suggestions, including key readings in the field, helped refine my arguments and broaden my perspective. I am also grateful to Daniel Silva for reading my proposal and providing very constructive feedback, which helped sharpen the focus of the project in its early stages. Any remaining shortcomings or errors are, of course, mine alone.

My gratitude goes to my colleague at Western Sydney University, Behrad Rezaei for our ongoing office discussions on Latour's Actor-Network Theory, and to Alex Luke for being a critical friend. Your input on the role of objects in everyday life has been invaluable. I am also thankful to Mahmud Hasan Khan for engaging with my analyses and pointing out areas that needed re-evaluation, helping me recognise and address potential biases. Your collective support has been instrumental in completing this Element. I would like to acknowledge the shop-owners and the customers who generously contributed their time and stories. Without them, this project, and others like it, would not have been possible.

Special thanks to my colleague/mentor, Sender Dovchin, for her constant support and encouragement during both the highs and lows of this journey. Thank you, Sender, your support has been invaluable. I would also like to acknowledge the collegiality and insightful conversations I've shared from time to time with Theo van Leeuwen, Alastair Pennycook, Adam Jaworski, Shaila Sultana, Emi Otsuji, Anna Cristina Pertierra, Alison M. Downham Moore, Ruying Qi, Robert Mailhammer, Alison Barnes, Peter Mauch, Saeed Rezaei, Hadi Mirvahedi, Nick Marshall, Stacey Sherwood, and Mahasta Zare.

Baala Vibi and Felinda Sharmal for their assistance with copyediting. Finally, to my family: to my wife, Hedi, who has always stood by me, and to my son, Aran, who regularly checked in to see what I was writing. I dedicate this Element to both of you. Your patience, curiosity, and emotional support have meant everything.

To my mum, whose encouragement never faltered, and to my father (watching from above) who instilled in me a deep respect for education: I think of you every day.

Cambridge Elements

Applied Linguistics

Li Wei
University College London

Li Wei is Chair of Applied Linguistics at the UCL Institute of Education, University College London (UCL), and Fellow of Academy of Social Sciences, UK. His research covers different aspects of bilingualism and multilingualism. He was the founding editor of the following journals: *International Journal of Bilingualism* (Sage), *Applied Linguistics Review* (De Gruyter), *Language, Culture and Society* (Benjamins), *Chinese Language and Discourse* (Benjamins) and *Global Chinese* (De Gruyter), and is currently Editor of the *International Journal of Bilingual Education and Bilingualism* (Taylor and Francis). His books include the *Blackwell Guide to Research Methods in Bilingualism and Multilingualism* (with Melissa Moyer) and *Translanguaging: Language, Bilingualism and Education* (with Ofelia Garcia) which won the British Association of Applied Linguistics Book Prize.

Zhu Hua
University College London

Zhu Hua is Professor of Language Learning and Intercultural Communication at the UCL Institute of Education, University College London (UCL) and is a Fellow of Academy of Social Sciences, UK. Her research is centred around multilingual and intercultural communication. She has also studied child language development and language learning. She is book series co-editor for *Routledge Studies in Language and Intercultural Communication* and *Cambridge Key Topics in Applied Linguistics*, and Forum and Book Reviews Editor of *Applied Linguistics* (Oxford University Press).

About the Series

Mirroring the Cambridge Key Topics in Applied Linguistics, this Elements series focuses on the key topics, concepts and methods in Applied Linguistics today. It revisits core conceptual and methodological issues in different subareas of Applied Linguistics. It also explores new emerging themes and topics. All topics are examined in connection with real-world issues and the broader political, economic and ideological contexts.

Cambridge Elements

Applied Linguistics

Elements in the Series

Second Language Pragmatics
Wei Ren

Kongish: Translanguaging and the Commodification of an Urban Dialect
Tong King Lee

Metalinguistic Awareness in Second Language Reading Development
Sihui Echo Ke, Dongbo Zhang and Keiko Koda

Crisis Leadership: Boris Johnson and Political Persuasion during the Covid Pandemic
Philip Seargeant

Writing Banal Inequalities: How to Fabricate Stories Which Disrupt
Edited by Hannah Cowan and Alfonso Del Percio

New Frontiers in Language and Technology
Christopher Joseph Jenks

Multimodality and Translanguaging in Video Interactions
Maria Grazia Sindoni

A Semiotics of Muslimness in China
Ibrar Bhatt

Narrative and Religion in the Superdiverse City
Stephen Pihlaja

Trans-studies on Writing for English as an Additional Language
Yachao Sun and Ge Lan

Investigating Plagiarism in Second Language Writing
Jun Lei and Guangwei Hu

Discourse, Materiality and Agency within Everyday Social Interactions
Dariush Izadi

A full series listing is available at www.cambridge.org/EIAL

For EU product safety concerns, contact us at Calle de José Abascal, 56–1°,
28003 Madrid, Spain or eugpsr@cambridge.org.

www.ingramcontent.com/pod-product-compliance
Lightning Source LLC
LaVergne TN
LVHW011853060526
838200LV00054B/4302